Nita Mehta's

101

MICROWAVE

❧ RECIPES ❧

Nita Mehta's

101

MICROWAVE

❧ RECIPES ❧

Nita Mehta

B.Sc. (Home Science), M.Sc. (Food & Nutrition) Gold Medalist

Tanya Mehta

SNAB
Excellence in Books

101
MICROWAVE
❦ RECIPES ❧

Snab Publishers Pvt Ltd

Corporate Office
3A/3, Asaf Ali Road, New Delhi 110 002
Phone: +91 11 2325 2948, 2325 0091
Telefax: +91 11 2325 0091
E-mail: nitamehta@nitamehta.com
Website: www.nitamehta.com

Editorial and Marketing office
E-159, Greater Kailash II, New Delhi 110 048

Food Styling and Photography by Snab
Typesetting by National Information Technology Academy
3A/3, Asaf Ali Road, New Delhi 110 002

Recipe Development & Testing:
Nita Mehta Foods - R & D Centre
3A/3, Asaf Ali Road, New Delhi - 110002
E-143, Amar Colony, Lajpat Nagar-IV, New Delhi - 110024

Distributed by :
NITA MEHTA BOOKS
3A/3, Asaf Ali Road, New Delhi - 02

Distribution Centre :
D16/1, Okhla Industrial Area, Phase-I,
New Delhi - 110020
Tel.: 26813199, 26813200
E-mail: nitamehta.mehta@gmail.com

NITA MEHTA BOOKS
Distributors & Publishers

NITA MEHTA FOODS

Price: Rs. 295/-

Introduction

The microwave helps today's women facing time constraints, to prepare a variety of favourite delicacies in a faster and a simpler manner. It leaves her with more time to spend with the family. Microwave makes the cooking simpler as the food does not stick or burn and hence it does not need constant stirring. The food is cooked and served in the

same dish, so there is less washing up to do. This effecient equipment not only reheats food but also boils, bakes, thaws and skewers, making cooking interesting and enjoyable. Microwave with its multiple advantages not only makes cooking much more fun, but also helps retain the food's nutritive value.

Cooking with microwave energy, is different from the conventional cooking. Microwaves are a form of high frequency electromagnetic waves which penetrate the food and execute the molecules inside, to vibrate at high speed. This causes friction and heat is produced thereby cooking the food very fast. The vitamins, the natural aroma and juices are retained, which invariably tends to get lost in conventional cooking. As the food is cooked in its own juices, very little oil or fat is used in cooking.

The recipes have been adapted to suit the Indian palate. This book covers a range of vegetarian and non vegetarian recipes, starting from starters to soups to main course Indian, Continental, Chinese and Thai dishes. A few desserts, some which turn out even better in a microwave than the conventional cooking, like our favourite "Gajar ka Halwah" have been made very simple to cook in a microwave. Look forward to these wonderful recipes and share it with those you love and care about!

Nita Mehta

Contents

SNACKS & STARTERS   13

SOUPS   30

INDIAN CURRIES   35

INDIAN DRY & MASALA   59

Dal Maharani 70
Bharwan Baingan 73
Mili-Juli-Subzi 74
Grilled Besani Subzi 76

Murg Amravati 71
Chicken Haldighati 72
Murg Jalfrezi 75
Mutton Keema 77

RICE 78

VEGETARIAN

Subz Pulao 80

NON-VEGETARIAN

Coconut Murg Pulao 79

CHINESE & THAI 81

VEGETARIAN

Honey Chilli Veggies 82
Paneer in Hot Garlic Sauce 84
Carrot Pepper Rice 86
Veggie Thai Red Curry 88

NON-VEGETARIAN

Chicken in Hot Garlic Sauce 83
Thai Green Curry 85
Dry Chilli Chicken 86
Stir Fried Schezwan Chicken 87

CONTINENTAL & BAKED DISHES 89

VEGETARIAN

Vegetable au Gratin 90
Stuffed Tomatoes 91
Rice-Vegetable Ring 93
Macaroni Alfredo 94
Bean Casserole 97
Hungarian Paneer 98

NON-VEGETARIAN

Chicken Potato Pie 92
Chicken Stroganoff 95
Chicken & Sweet Corn 96

DESSERTS & CAKES 99

WITHOUT EGGS

Gajar ka Halwa 100
Phirni 101
Lychee Pearls in Shahi Kheer 104
Eggless Cake with Mocha Icing 107

WITH EGGS

Pina Orange Dome 102
Coconut Pudding 103
Creme Caramel 105
Vanilla Cake 106
Chocolate Cake 106

HEALTHY OLIVE OIL RECIPES 108

Mini Corn Buns 109
Baby Corn Jalfrazie 110
Mushroom Olive Baskets 111
Herb Bread Loaf 112
Cottage Cheese Steaks 113
Quick Tandoori Platter 114

Spinach Paneer Casserole 115
Baked Yogurt Wheels 116
Riec & Corn Salad 117
Grilled Cheesy Bites 118
Veggie Pepper Rice 119
Creamed Corn Chillies 120

Herbs & Spices

	ENGLISH NAME		HINDI NAME
1	Sesame Seeds	1	तिल
2	Mustrad Seeds	2	राई, सरसों
3	Melon Seeds	3	खरबूज़े के बीज
4	Coriander Seeds	4	साबुत धनिया
5	Coriander Seeds, Ground	5	धनिया पाउडर
6	Mango Powder	6	अमचूर
7	Red Chilli Powder	7	लाल मिर्च पाउडर
8	Cumin Seeds, White	8	जीरा
9	Carom Seeds	9	अजवाइन
10	Fennel	10	सौंफ
11	Cumin Seeds, Black	11	शाह जीरा
12	Garam Masala - A Spice Blend	12	गरम मसाला
13	Asafoetida	13	हींग
14	Saffron	14	केसर
15	Fenugreek Leaves, Dried	15	कसूरी मेथी
16	Fenugreek Seeds	16	मेथी दाना
17	Pomegranate Seeds, Dried	17	अनार दाना
18	Nigella Seeds	18	कलौंजी
19	Turmeric	19	हल्दी
20	Cloves	20	लौंग
21	Nutmeg	21	जयफल
22	Peppercorns	22	साबुत काली मिर्च
23	Black Cardamom	23	मोटी इलाइची
24	Green Cardmamom	24	छोटी इलाइची
25	Mace	25	जावित्री
26	Cinnamon	26	दालचीनी
27	Fresh Green Chillies	27	हरी मिर्च
28	Red Chillies, Dried	28	सूखी लाल मिर्च
29	Ginger	29	अदरक
30	Garlic	30	लहसुन
31	Coriander, Fresh	31	हरा धनिया
32	Bay Leaves	32	तेज पत्ता
33	Curry Leaves	33	करी पत्ता
34	Mint	34	पुदीना

Microwave Tips

- Never over-cook food as it becomes tough and leathery. Give the dish a little standing time before you test it, to avoid over cooking.
- Never pile food on top of each other. It cooks better, evenly and quickly when spaced apart.
- Food cooks better in a round container than in a square one. In square or rectangular bowls, the food gets overcooked at the corners.
- Do not add salt at the time of starting the cooking as it leads to increase in the cooking time.
- Do not add more water than required, however a little water must be added to prevent dehydration of the vegetables. When the vegetables get dehydrated, there is a loss of natural juices as well. But addition of extra water increases the cooking time.
- Do not deep fry in a microwave (the temperature of oil cannot be controlled).
- Do not cook eggs in their shells (pressure will cause them to explode).
- Do not cook & reheat puddings having alcohol (they can easily catch fire).
- Do not use containers with restricted openings, such as bottles.
- Use deep dishes to prepare gravies, filling the dish only ¾ to avoid spillage.
- Do not use aluminium foil for covering dishes in the microwave mode. Do not reheat foods (sweets like ladoos, burfi etc.) with silver sheet, as it leads to sparking.
- When using the convec mode put the dish on the wire rack to get even baking.
- Always preheat the oven when you want to use the convec mode. Grilling does not always need preheating, but preheating hastens the browning.
- When making tikkas or other tandoori delicacies cover the plate beneath the rack with aluminiun foil to collect the drippings.

Interesting Uses of Microwave

- Making ghee. Keep 1½ - 2 cups malai (milk topping) in a big glass bowl and microwave on high for 15-20 minutes to get desi ghee without burning your kadhai (wok). Stir once or twice inbetween.

- Blanching almonds to remove skin. Put almonds in a small bowl of water and microwave for 3 minutes or till water just starts to boil. After the water cools, the almonds can be peeled very easily.

- Freshening stale chips, biscuits or cornflakes. Place the chips or biscuits on a napkin, uncovered, for about 1 minute per bowl or until they feel warm. Wait for a few minutes to allow cooling and serve.

- Boiling (actually microwaving) potatoes. Wash potatoes. Place them on the turntable. Microwave covered for 5 minutes for 4 medium potatoes.

- Making khatti mithi chutney. Mix 1 tbsp amchur, 3 tbsp sugar, ¼ cup water along with spices in a glass bowl. Microwave for 3 minutes stirring in between.

- Warming baby's milk bottle. Do check the temperature of the milk on your inner wrist. The bottle will not become hot, while the milk will.

- Softening too-hard ice cream, cream, cheese and butter.

- Making dry bread crumbs from fresh bread. Crumble the slice of bread and microwave the bits of slices for 2-3 minutes. Mix once and microwave further for another minute or two. Give some standing time to the moist bread to dry out and then grind in a mixer to get crumbs.

- Drying herbs. Fresh parsley, dill (soye), mint (poodina), coriander (dhaniyan), fenugreek greens (methi) — all greens can be dried in a microwave, preserving the green colour. Give them some standing time to turn dry. Use them in raitas and curries.

- Melting chocolate, butter, jam, honey, etc. Dissolving gelatine.

- Sterilizing jars for storing home made jams and pickles.

Cookware Selection Guide

MODE	CAN USE	DO NOT USE
### Microwave Round or oval dishes are recommended for this mode as the corners of the square dish absorb more microwave energy or rays and hence food at the corners tends to get over cooked.	China Pottery (earthenware) Heatproof glass dishes like pyrex, borosil etc. Paper and cloth napkins as covers Plastic or cling wrap can be used as cover for short durations. Wooden skewers and toothpicks Plastic or polythene cooking bags.	China or any other utensil with gold or silver lining. Very delicate glass dishes Metal cake tins or any other metal Aluminium foil as covers Metal skewers
### Convection This terminology utilizes a heater and metal fan to circulate hot air in the cavity. The oven becomes a conventional oven when put on this mode so all utensils which go in the regular oven work well in the microwave oven when set on the convection mode.	Metal cake tins or any other metal utensil Heat proof glass dishes like pyrex or borosil Metal skewers Aluminium foil as covers	Delicate glass dishes which are not heatproof Wooden skewers Paper and cloth napkins or plastic wraps
### Grill In this mode there are no microwaves so all heatproof utensils work well.	Same as convection mode	Same as convection mode
### Combination (Micro+convec) (Micro+Grill) Utensils must be microproof as well as heatproof for both the combination modes	Heat proof glass dishes like pyrex or borosil Use a glass microproof and heatproof glass plate as cover	Metal tins China Wooden and metal skewers Aluminium foil, paper or cloth napkins or plastic wrap.
### Combination (Grill+Convec) Utensils must be heatproof	Same as convection mode	Same as convection mode

SNACKS & STARTERS

Chicken Tikka

Chunks of marinated chicken cooked in the microwave to give soft and succulent tikkas.

Serve 4

INGREDIENTS

350 gm boneless chicken - 1" pieces

some chaat masala and lemon juice

2 tbsp melted butter - to baste

MARINADE (MIX TOGETHER)

1 cup curd - hang in a cloth for 30 minutes

2 tbsp thick malai or cream or oil

2 tsp ginger-garlic paste

¾ tsp tandoori masala (optional)

¼ tsp black salt (kala namak), ½ tsp garam masala powder

½ tsp red chilli powder

1 tsp salt

2-3 drops of tandoori red colour

METHOD

1   Hang curd in a muslin cloth for 30 minutes to drain out the liquid.

2   Cut chicken into 1" pieces. Wash chicken and pat dry on a napkin.

3   Marinate the pieces in the marinade for atleast 2-3 hours or longer and keep in the fridge till serving time.

4   Set the microwave oven at 180°C using the oven (convection) mode and press start to preheat oven.

5   Grease the wire rack or grill rack. Put the tikkas on the greased rack and place it in the hot oven.

6   Set the preheated oven for 20 minutes. Cook the tikkas for 15 minutes. Spoon some melted butter on the tikkas and cook further for 5 minutes or until cooked. Remove from oven.

7   Sprinkle chat masala & lemon juice. Serve hot.

Dakshini Crispies

Enjoy the South Indian style topping on crisp pieces of bread.

Serves 4

INGREDIENTS

3 bread slices

1 potato

2 tbsp suji (semolina)

½ tsp salt, or to taste

¼ tsp pepper, or to taste

½ onion - very finely chopped

½ tomato - cut into half, deseeded and chopped finely

2 tbsp curry leaves - chopped

½ tsp rai (small brown mustard seeds)

METHOD

1 Wash potato. Microwave covered for 3 minutes. Peel and mash coarsely.

2 To the mashed potatoes, add onion, tomato, curry leaves, salt and pepper. Mix the ingredients.

3 Add the suji and mix lightly.

4 Spread potato mixture carefully on bread slices, keeping edges neat.

5 Sprinkle some rai over the potato mixture, pressing down gently with finger tips.

6 Keep the bread slices in the microwave oven on the combination mode (convec+grill) and cook for 15 minutes or till the bottom of the slice gets crisp.

7 Cut each toast into 4 triangular or square pieces. Serve with tomato ketchup or mustard sauce.

Methi Mahi Tikka

The healthy fish tikkas made more delicious with mint and fenugreek.

Serve 4-6

INGREDIENTS

500 gm boneless fish - cut into 2" cubes

3 tbsp gram flour (besan), 1 tbsp lemon juice

1ST MARINADE

2 tbsp vinegar or lemon juice, ¼ tsp red chilli powder, ½ tsp salt

GRIND TO A FINE PASTE

1 tbsp mint leaves, 1 tbsp kasoori methi

1" piece of ginger, 5-6 flakes garlic

2ND MARINADE

¼ cup thick cream, ½ cup curd - hang in a muslin cloth for ½ hr

3 tbsp cheese - finely grated

½ tsp green cardamom (illaichi) powder

2 tbsp cornflour, 1 tbsp oil, 3 cloves (laung) - crushed

1 tsp salt, 1 tsp red chilli powder

METHOD

1. Rub the fish well with besan and lemon juice. Keep aside for 15 minutes. Wash and pat dry on a kitchen towel. Marinate fish with all ingredients of the 1st marinade. Keep aside ½ hour.

2. Drain, wash and pat dry with a towel.

3. Grind all ingredients of paste.

4. Rub the tikkas thoroughly with the paste. Keep aside for ½ hour.

5. Mix ingredients of 2nd marinade.

6. Add tikka pieces to this marinade and coat well. Keep aside for 3 hours.

7. Brush grill rack of the oven with oil.

8. Place the tikka pieces on it and put them in the microwave oven on the combination mode (micro+grill) and cook for 15 minutes till coating turns dry and golden brown.

Chutney Submarine

Mango chutney spread on a loaf of bread and topped with some salad and paneer roundels.

Serves 4-5

INGREDIENTS

1 long French bread - cut lengthwise

2 tbsp butter - softened

2 tbsp sweet mango chutney

1 cucumber - cut into round slices without peeling

2 firm tomatoes - cut into round slices

a few poodina (mint) leaves to garnish

400 gm paneer

2 tbsp oil

¼ tsp haldi

½ tsp chilli powder

½ tsp salt

1 tsp chaat masala powder

METHOD

1   Cut paneer into ¼" thick slices and then into round pieces with a biscuit cutter or bottle cover or into squares.

2   Sprinkle paneer on both sides with some chilli powder, salt, haldi, chaat masala and oil. Grill for 10 minutes.

3   Spread butter on the cut surface of both the pieces of french bread, as well as a little on the sides.

4   Set your microwave oven at 180°C using the oven (convection) mode and press start to preheat oven.

5   Place bread on grill rack in the hot oven. Set the preheated oven 12 minutes. Cook till bread turns crisp.

6   Apply 2 tbsp chutney on the crispy buttered side.

7   Sprinkle some chaat masala crisp on the cucumber and tomato pieces.

8   Place a piece of paneer, then cucumber, then tomato and keep repeating all three in the same sequence so as to cover the loaf. Place them slightly overlapping. Insert fresh mint leaves in between the vegetables, for garnishing. Serve at room temperature.

Spicy Seekh Pizza

A quick and crisp pizza made by using readymade seekh kebabs.

Makes 2

INGREDIENTS

2 readymade chicken seekhs - cut into ¼" thick slices and then mix with 1½ tbsp oil

2 ready-made pizza bases

150 gm pizza cheese - grated (1½ cups)

½ onion - chopped, 1 tomato - chopped

1 small capsicum - chopped

½ tsp each of salt, orgeano & chilli flakes

TOMATO SPREAD

4 flakes garlic - crushed

½ cup ready made tomato puree, 2 tbsp tomato sauce

¼ tsp salt, ¼ tsp pepper to taste

½ tsp red chilli powder, ½ tsp oregano

METHOD

1   To prepare tomato spread, put 2 tbsp oil, garlic, tomato puree, sauce, salt, pepper, red chilli powder & oregano in a microproof bowl. Mix well. Microwave for 4 minutes.

2   Mix onion, capsicum, tomato, salt, pepper and oregano in a bowl.

3   Spread tomato spread on each pizza base. Spread ½ the chopped vegetables on each base. Sprinkle ½ of the cheese on each base. Top each with ½ of the seekh slices. Sprinkle red chilli flakes on the seekhs.

4   Set microwave oven at 240°C using oven (convection) mode and press start to preheat the oven.

5   Put the pizza on the wire rack in the preheated oven and then cook for 10 minutes or more, till the base gets crisp.

Tomato Kaju Idli

The regular South Indian idlis made more appetizing!

Make 6 Idlis

INGREDIENTS

1 cup suji (rawa)

1½ tbsp oil

1 cup curd

½ cup water, approx.

½ tsp soda-bicarb

¾ tsp salt

OTHER INGREDIENTS

1 firm tomato - cut into 8 slices

4-5 cashews - split into halves

8-10 curry leaves

METHOD

1   In a dish put 1½ tbsp oil. Microwave for 1 minute.

2   Add suji. Mix well. Microwave uncovered for 2 minutes.

3   Add salt. Mix well. Allow to cool.

4   Add curd and water. Mix till smooth.

5   Add soda-bicarb. Mix very well till smooth. Keep aside for 10 minutes.

6   Grease 6 small glass katoris or plastic idli boxes. Arrange a slice of tomato, a split cashew half and a curry leaf at the bottom of the katori.

7   Pour 3-4 tbsp mixture into each katori.

8   Arrange katoris in a ring in the microwave and microwave uncovered for 3½ minutes.

9   Let them stand for 5 minutes. Serve hot with sambhar and chutney.

Pav Bhaji

Mixed vegetables flavoured with a fragrant spice blend. Enjoy it as a snack or for dinner.

Serve 4

INGREDIENTS

3 onions - chopped finely

3 potatoes

2 carrots - peeled and chopped

½ cup peas

1½ cups chopped cauliflower

1 cup chopped cabbage

3 tbsp oil

3 tbsp butter

2 tsp ginger-garlic paste

2½ tbsp pav bhaji masala

¼ tsp haldi (turmeric powder)

1½ tsp salt

3 tomatoes - chopped

1 tbsp chopped coriander

METHOD

1. Wash potatoes. Microwave covered for 5 minutes. Peel and mash coarsely.

2. In a deep microproof bowl, put carrots, peas, cauliflower and cabbage. Add ½ cup water. Mix and microwave for 8 minutes. Let it cool. Blend roughly in a mixer for 1-2 seconds. Do not make it into a paste.

3. In a microproof dish add oil, onions, ginger-garlic paste, 2 tbsp pav bhaji masala and haldi. Mix well. Microwave for 6 minutes.

4. Add tomatoes and the roughly mashed vegetables. Mix well. Add 2 tbsp butter, 1½ tsp salt. Cover and microwave for 10 minutes. Stir once in between.

5. Add 1 cup water. Mix and microwave for 5 minutes.

6. Add 1 tsp pav bhaji masala, 1 tbsp chopped coriander and 1 tbsp butter. Mix and serve.

Bean Squares

A quick Mexican starter - crackers topped with cheesy beans and roasted peanuts.

Serves 4

INGREDIENTS

8 cream cracker biscuits

½ cup grated cheese

½ cup boiled rajmah (red kidney beans)

2 tbsp tomato sauce

½ tsp salt, ¼ tsp red chilli powder

2 green chillies - deseeded, finely chopped

½ tsp oregano, ½ tsp salt

a few roasted peanuts

SOUR CREAM

2 tbsp fresh cream - chilled

½ cup thick dahi (yogurt) - hang for 15 minutes in a muslin cloth & squeeze lightly

½ tsp lemon juice, ¼ tsp salt, or to taste

¼ tsp pepper, preferably white pepper

METHOD

1. For the sour cream, beat curd till smooth. Gently mix lemon juice, cream, salt and pepper. Keep sour cream in the refrigerator till serving time.

2. Mix cheese, boiled rajmah, tomato sauce, salt, red chilli powder and chopped green chillies. Keep topping aside till serving time.

3. To serve, spread 1 tbsp full of the bean topping on each biscuit in a heap, leaving the edges clean.

4. Place a paper napkin on the glass plate in the microwave.

5. Keep all the cream cracker biscuits together on it and microwave at 60% power for 3 minutes.

6. Serve each biscuit with a blob of sour cream and then top with a peanut.

Khandvi

Light and delicious gramflour rolls stuffed with fresh coconut.

Serves 6-8

INGREDIENTS

½ cup gram flour (besan)

1¾ cups butter milk (mix ¾ cup curd with 1 cup water)

¼ tsp haldi, ¼ tsp cumin (jeera) powder

½ tsp coriander powder

a pinch asafoetida (hing) , 1 tsp salt, ½ tsp sugar

1 big (12") thali or tray - greased with oil on the back side

a flat bottom katori - grease the bottom

PASTE

½" piece ginger, 1-2 green chillies

TEMPERING

1½ tbsp oil, ½ tsp mustard seeds (rai), 2-3 green chillies

few coriander leaves

few curry leaves

FILLING

2-3 tbsp freshly grated coconut

METHOD

1   Mix besan with buttermilk in a flat dish till smooth. Microwave uncovered for 4 minutes. Stir. Add all other ingredients and ginger green chilli paste and microwave for 4 min. Stir & microwave for 2 minutes.

2   Spread mixture thinly on the back of a greased tray or kitchen platform while it is hot. Immediately level it with the back of a katori which is greased well.

3   Cut into 1½-2" wide strips and 7 inches long. Sprinkle coconut. Roll each strip to get small cylinders.

4   Mix all ingredients of tempering and microwave for 3 minutes. Pour on the khandvi. Serve.

Paneer Tikka

The universal Indian delight, now made more delicious!

Serves 4

INGREDIENTS

300 gm paneer- cut into 2" squares

1 large capsicum - cut into 1" pieces

1 onion - cut into 4 pieces

1 tomato - cut into 8 pieces

MARINADE

1 cup yogurt (dahi) - hang in a muslin cloth for 30 minutes

3 tbsp thick malai or thick cream

a few drops of orange colour or a pinch of turmeric (haldi)

1½ tbsp oil

1 tbsp cornflour

½ tsp amchoor ½ tsp black salt

½ tsp red chilli powder

¾ tsp salt

1 tbsp tandoori or chicken masala

1 tbsp ginger-garlic paste

METHOD

1   Mix all ingredients of the marinade in a bowl. Add paneer. Mix well.

2   Grease wire or grill rack. Arrange paneer on the greased wire rack. After all the paneer pieces are done, put capsicum, onions and tomato together in the left over marinade and mix well to coat the vegetables. Place vegetables also on the rack.

3   Set your microwave oven at 200°C using the oven (convection) mode and press start to preheat.

4   Put the tikkas in the hot oven.

5   Set the preheated oven for 15 minutes. Cook the tikkas for 15 minutes.

6   Spoon some melted butter on the tikkas and grill for 5 minutes. Remove from oven. Sprinkle chat masala & lemon juice. Serve hot.

Shami Kebab

Small patties of mince meat, grilled in the microwave to perfection.

Makes 15 kebabs

INGREDIENTS

½ kg mutton mince (keema)

1 onion - sliced

10 flakes garlic - chopped, 2" piece ginger - chopped

2 tsp saboot dhania (coriander seeds)

1 tsp cumin seeds (jeera), 3-4 cloves (laung)

seeds of 2 green cardamom (illaichi)

seeds of 1 black cardamom

½" stick cinnamon (dalchini)

4-5 whole peppercorns

2-3 dry, whole red chillies

salt to taste, ½ cup water

1- 2 green chillies - chopped, 1 egg, 4 tbsp besan (gramflour)

1 tbsp kasoori methi

1 tbsp chopped coriander

METHOD

1   Wash the mince in a strainer and press well to drain out the water well through the strainer.

2   Except egg, besan, kasoori methi and coriander, add all ingredients to the mince in a shallow microproof dish and mix very well. Microwave at 70% power for 10 minutes.

3   Grind mince in a mixer without adding any water till smooth.

4   Mix egg, besan, kasoori methi and coriander.

5   Take a ball of the mixture, shape into a ball and flatten it to give a shape of a kebab/disc with oiled hands.

6   Grill for 20 minutes on the rack. After 10 minutes, overturn the kebabs and pour ½ tsp oil on each kebab and grill for another 10 minutes. Serve hot with hari chutney.

Instant Khaman Dhokla

This light Gujarati snack is quick to make in a microwave.

Serves 6

INGREDIENTS

1½ cups besan (gram flour)

1 cup water

1 tbsp oil

½ tsp turmeric (haldi)

1 tsp green chilli paste, 1 tsp ginger paste

1 tsp salt

1 tsp sugar

¼ tsp soda-bi-carb (mitha soda)

1½ tsp eno fruit salt, 2 tsp lemon juice

TEMPERING

2 tbsp oil, 1 tsp mustard seeds (rai)

2-3 green chillies - slit into long pieces

2 tbsp white vinegar

¾ cup water, 1 tbsp sugar

METHOD

1   Grease a 7" diameter round, flat dish with oil. Keep aside.

2   Sift besan through sieve to make it light and free of any lumps.

3   Mix besan, water, oil, turmeric powder, salt, sugar, chilli paste, ginger paste and water to a smooth batter.

4   Add eno fruit salt and soda-bi-carb to the batter and pour lemon juice over it. Beat well for a few seconds.

5   Immediately pour this mixture in the greased dish. Microwave uncovered for 6 minutes. Remove from oven and keep aside.

6   To temper, microwave oil, green chillies and rai for 2½ minutes. Add water, sugar and vinegar and microwave for 4½ minutes. Pour over the dhokla and wait for ½ hour so that dhokla absorbs water and turns soft.

7   Cool and cut into 1½" pieces.

8   Sprinkle chopped coriander. Serve.

Crispy Chicken

Chicken coated with bread crumbs and grilled till crisp and succulent.

Serves 4

INGREDIENTS

400 gms chicken drumsticks (small legs)

MARINADE

4 tbsp oil or melted butter

1½ tsp garlic paste

1½ tsp chilli powder

1 tsp jeera (cumin seeds) - powdered

2 tsp dhania powder (coriander powder)

2" stick dalchini (cinnamon) - powdered

1 tbsp maida (flour)

1½ tsp salt

OTHER INGREDIENTS

2 eggs - beat well, ½ cup dry bread crumbs

METHOD

1   Wash chicken, pat dry on a cloth napkin. Prick with a fork all over.

2   Mix all the ingredients written under marinade in a flat bowl.

3   Add the chicken & let it marinate for 4 hours or overnight in the fridge. (The longer the marination time, the more flavourful the chicken).

4   Beat eggs lightly. Add ¼ tsp salt and ¼ tsp red chilli powder. Mix well.

5   Spread bread crumbs in a flat plate.

6   Dip each chicken leg in egg and roll it in the bread crumbs.

7   Set your microwave oven at 200°C using the oven (convection) mode and press start to preheat.

8   Place chicken in a baking dish, pour 1 tbsp oil or melted butter on the pieces and place in the hot oven.

9   Set the hot oven for 40 minutes. First, bake for 20 minutes. Then overturn the pieces and sprinkle 1 tbsp of butter on the legs. Bake for the remaining 20 minutes or till chicken is cooked.

Chicken Rolls

Soft and creamy rolls are low in calories too.

Makes 6-7 small rolls

INGREDIENTS

200 gms chicken with bones

½ onion - chopped

1 tbsp oil

1 tbsp butter

1 tbsp maida (flour)

¼ cup milk

½ tsp salt

¼ tsp pepper or to taste

¼ tsp red chilli flakes

2 green chillies - chopped

1 bread slice - churned in a mixer

1 egg, ½ cup maida (flour)

METHOD

1   Put chicken and 1 tbsp oil in a microproof bowl. Microwave covered for 5 minutes. Shred chicken into very small pieces. Remove chicken from dish. Discard bones.

2   Melt butter for 30 seconds in the same microproof dish.

3   Add shredded chicken, onion, salt, pepper, red chilli flakes, green chillies and maida. Microwave for 20 seconds.

4   Add milk, mix well and microwave uncovered for 1 minute. Remove from microwave.

5   Add freshly churned bread crumbs. Keeping aside 2 tbsp of egg white add the rest of the egg to the chicken mixture. Check salt. Mix well.

6   Shape the mixture into 6-7 rolls. Flatten the sides by pressing the sides against a flat surface.

7   Mix 2 tbsp egg white with 2 tbsp of water. Dip each roll in it & then roll over maida spread in a plate. Coat well. Keep in the fridge.

8   To serve, grill for 20 minutes till the rolls turn golden brown and crisp. Overturn in between after 10 minutes. Serve hot with ketchup.

Chicken Sandwiches

Chicken shreds in mayonnaise spiked with mustard make wonderful grilled sandwiches.

Serves 4-6

INGREDIENTS

1 chicken breast with bones

8 bread slices, preferably brown bread

½ onion - cut into very thin slices and separated

5-6 tbsp ready-made mayonnaise

½ tsp salt

½ tsp pepper

½ tsp oregano

1 tsp mustard sauce (ready-made)

2 tbsp butter - to spread on bread slices

a few lettuce or cabbage leaves

METHOD

1   Put chicken and oil in a microproof dish and microwave covered for 3 minutes. Remove from microwave. Cool and debone the chicken from the bones and shred into very small pieces.

2   In a bowl mix together chicken pieces, onion, mayonnaise, salt, pepper, oregano and mustard. Check seasonings. Keep the seasonings of the filling a little strong because it may taste bland when applied on the bread.

3   Butter each bread slice on one side.

4   Spread the chicken mixture on the unbuttered side of the bread slice. Break lettuce or cabbage leaf into bite size pieces and place on filling.

5   Top with another slice, keeping the buttered side outside. Repeat with other slices to make 4 sandwiches.

6   Put sandwich on the wire rack. Press well on the rack to get lines on the sandwiches. Grill for 7-8 minutes. Inbetween, after 4-5 minutes, turn side and grilll till both sides are crisp and golden.

Sesame Gold Coins

Sesame seeds and vegetables on golden brown bread, dotted with some tomato ketchup.

Servings 12

INGREDIENTS

6 bread slices

butter enough to spread, 1 tbsp oil

2 potatoes

1 small onion - chopped finely

1 carrot - chopped finely (diced)

1 capsicum - chopped finely (diced)

½ tsp soya sauce, 1 tsp vinegar

½ tsp pepper

¼ tsp chilli powder

salt to taste

sesame seeds (til) - to sprinkle

chilli garlic tomato sauce to dot

METHOD

1   Wash potatoes. Microwave covered for 4 minutes. Peel and mash coarsely.

2   In a dish microwave onion and oil for 3 minutes. Add vegetables. Microwave for 2 minutes.

3   Add potatoes, soya sauce, vinegar, salt, pepper and chilli powder. Microwave for 2 minutes.

4   With a cutter or a sharp lid, cut out small rounds (about 1½" diameter) of the bread. Butter both sides of each piece lightly.

5   Spread some potato mixture in a slight heap on the round piece of bread, leaving the edges clean. Press. Sprinkle sesame seeds. Press.

6   Set your microwave oven at 180°C using the oven (convection) mode and press start to preheat oven.

7   Place gold coins on grill rack.

8   Re-set the preheated oven at 180°C for 12 minutes. Cook till bread turns golden on the edges and turns crisp from the under side. Serve, dotted with chilli-garlic sauce.

SOUPS

Sweet Corn Soup

The all time favourite Chinese soup!

Serve 4

INGREDIENTS

150 gm chicken with bones

2 whole corns-on-the cob (bhutta)

¼ cup cabbage - shredded

½ cup grated carrot

2 tbsp butter

3 tbsp cornflour- dissolve in ½ cup water

2 tbsp white vinegar

1 tbsp sugar

½ tsp ajinomoto (optional)

½ tsp white pepper

1½ tsp salt

1-2 drops soya sauce

METHOD

1 Wash and microwave chicken covered with ½ cup water at 70% power for 6 minutes. Remove chicken from the bones.

2 Remove husk from corn and break each into 2 pieces. Put the corn pieces in a ploythene bag (plastic bag), tie the mouth of the bag loosely and microwave for 4½ minutes.

3 Scrape corn from the cob with a knife. Churn corn roughly in a mixer with ½ cup water for a few seconds.

4 Put the crushed corn, 4 cups of water, 1½ tsp salt, vinegar, pepper and sugar. Add butter. Mix well and microwave covered for 8 minutes. Stir once inbetween.

5 Dissolve cornflour in ½ cup water & add to the soup. Microwave covered for 3 minutes. Stir once in between.

6 Add cabbage and carrot. Add boiled chicken, along with the liquid and soya sauce. Mix well. Check salt. Microwave for 1 minute.

7 Serve hot with green chillies in vinegar.

Chicken Mulligatawny

Chicken soup with pepper and coconut milk as the main ingredients.

Serves 4-6

INGREDIENTS

250 gm chicken with bones

2 cups coconut milk (ready made)

1 onion - chopped

a few curry leaves

3-4 flakes garlic - crushed

½" piece ginger - finely chopped

½ tsp roasted cumin (jeera) powder

½ tsp turmeric (haldi) powder

½ tsp red chilli powder, ½ tsp pepper

1 large tomato, salt to taste

TO GARNISH

2 tbsp boiled rice

METHOD

1   Wash and microwave covered, chicken and 2 cups water for 6 minutes. Strain.

2   Reserve the strained liquid.

3   Shred and keep the chicken aside and discard the bones.

4   Put a cross on the stem end of tomato and microwave for 1½ minutes in a plate. After it cools, remove peel and chop finely.

5   Microwave 1 tbsp oil, onion, curry leaves, garlic, ginger, cumin, haldi, chilli powder and pepper for 4 minutes.

6   Add the chopped tomato, salt, coconut milk, shredded chicken. and the strained liquid. The soup should now be 4 cups in quantity. Microwave for 10 minutes, stirring once in between.

7   Pour soup into bowls and garnish with a tsp of boiled rice. Serve hot.

Capsicum Soup

A cheesy light green soup.

Serves 4

INGREDIENTS

4 medium sized capsicums - cut into big pieces

2 tomatoes - cut into big pieces

2 cups water

½ cup milk

2 tsp cheese spread

1 tsp salt

½ tsp pepper or to taste

1 tsp butter

METHOD

1   Microwave capsicum and tomato with 1 cup water in a microproof bowl for 3 minutes.

2   Remove from the microwave, cool.

3   Add 1 cup water. Churn in a mixer to get a smooth puree. Strain puree.

4   To the strained puree add milk, cheese spread, salt, pepper and butter. Microwave for 6 minutes.

5   Pour into individual bowls and serve hot.

Corn Minestrone

A hearty Italian tomato soup with vegetables.

Serves 4-6

INGREDIENTS

½ cup corn kernels

2 mushrooms - sliced very finely

¼ cup finely chopped carrots

1 tbsp finely chopped french beans

¼ cup finely chopped potatoes

2 large tomatoes

1 tbsp butter

2 tbsp chopped onions

5 cups water mixed with a seasoning cube

salt and pepper to taste

GARNISH

2-3 tbsp grated cheese

METHOD

1   To blanch the tomatoes, put a cross on the stem end of each tomato and place on a microproof plate. Microwave for 2 minutes. Peel the skin & chop them finely.

2   Put butter in a big, deep microproof bowl. Microwave for 30 seconds.

3   Add onions and microwave for 2 minutes.

4   Add corn, mushrooms, carrots, french beans and potatoes. Mix well. Microwave for 5 minutes.

5   Add blanched and chopped tomatoes, pepper and water mixed with a vegetarian seasoning cube. Microwave covered for 8 minutes. Stir once inbetween.

6   Remove from the microwave and mash lightly. Check salt.

7   Serve hot in soup bowls garnished with finely grated cheese.

INDIAN CURRIES

Palak Paneer

Spinach and cottage cheese - a wonderful combination!

Serve 4

INGREDIENTS

250 gm paneer - cut into 1" cubes

1 bundle (600 gm) spinach

2 tbsp oil, 1 tsp cumin seeds (jeera)

½" piece ginger, 4-5 flakes of garlic

2 onions - chopped, 1 green chilli - chopped

2 tsp coriander powder (dhania powder)

½ tsp garam masala

2 tomatoes - chopped

2 tbsp dry fenugreek leaves (kasoori methi)

1 tbsp butter, ½ tsp red chilli powder

¾ tsp salt, ¼ tsp sugar

¼ cup milk

METHOD

1. In a microproof deep bowl put oil, jeera, ginger, garlic, onions, green chilli, 2 tsp dhania powder and garam masala. Mix well. Microwave for 5 minutes.

2. Add chopped tomatoes and kasoori methi. Mix well. Add washed spinach leaves. Microwave for 8 minutes.

3. Cool spinach. Blend with ½ cup water.

4. Transfer the spinach puree to the same microproof dish. Add 1 tbsp butter, ½ tsp red chilli powder, paneer, ¾ tsp salt, ¼ tsp sugar, ¼ cup milk and ¼ cup water. Mix well.

5. Microwave for 5 minutes. Serve hot.

Carrot Kofta Curry

Carrot balls stuffed with raisins in a simple, yet tasty curry.

Serves 4

INGREDIENTS

3 tbsp oil

2 onions - ground to a paste in a mixer

2 tomatoes - pureed in a mixer

2 tsp dhania powder

¼ tsp haldi

¼ tsp garam masala

¼ tsp red chilli powder

KOFTE

2 carrots - grated

2 bread slices - break into pieces and grind to crumbs in a mixer

1 green chilli - chopped

1 tsp ginger paste, ½ tsp salt

¼ tsp of each - garam masala, amchoor and red chilli powder

2 tbsp yogurt/curd

8-10 kishmish

METHOD

1   For the gravy, mix onion paste with oil, haldi, dhania powder, garam masala and red chilli powder in a deep microproof dish. Microwave for 8 minutes.

2   Add pureed tomatoes. Microwave for 7 minutes.

3   Add 1½ cups water. Microwave for 6 minutes. Keep aside.

4   For the koftas, mix carrots with all ingredients of the koftas except yogurt and kishmish.

5   Add yogurt. Mix well. Make 8 round balls with 1 kishmish stuffed in each. Place balls on a greased microproof plate in a ring and microwave for 3 minutes.

6   At serving time, place koftas in a serving dish. Pour curry over them. Microwave for 2 minutes and serve.

Butter Chicken

Tandoori chicken in a red cashew based makhani gravy.

Serve 4

INGREDIENTS

1 medium sized chicken (800 gm) - cut into 12 pieces

juice of 1 lemon, ½ tsp chilli powder, 1¼ tsp salt, or to taste

MARINADE

¾ cup curd - hang for 30 minutes in a muslin cloth

1 tbsp cornflour, 1 tbsp grated onion, ½ tsp black salt

2 tbsp thick cream, 1 tbsp ginger- garlic paste

1 tbsp kasoori methi (dry fenugreek leaves)

few drops of orange red colour, 1 tsp garam masala

PASTE

2" piece of ginger, 10 flakes of garlic

2 cups readymade tomato puree, 4 tbsp (cashewnuts)

1 tsp garam masala, ½ tsp chilli powder, ¼ tsp sugar, ½ tsp salt

OTHER INGREDIENTS

1 cup milk, 2 tbsp cream, 2 tbsp butter, 2-3 tbsp oil

METHOD

1   Wash, pat dry chicken. Prick all pieces with a fork on all sides. Rub lemon juice, salt and chilli powder on the chicken and keep aside for ½ hour.

2   Mix all the ingredients of the marinade well. Add chicken and mix well. Keep aside for 3-4 hours in the fridge.

3   Set microwave oven at 180°C using convection mode and press start to preheat. Grease wire rack. Put chicken pieces on the greased rack and place it in hot oven. Place a tray covered with foil in the oven, underneath the chicken to collect drippings.

4   Set the preheated oven for 20 minutes. Cook the pieces for 20 minutes or till cooked. Remove from oven. Keep tandoori chicken aside.

5   Grind all the ingredients of paste to a smooth paste in a mixer.

6   For gravy, put butter, oil and the prepared paste in a microproof bowl. Mix well and microwave for 8 minutes.

7   Add about 1½ cups of water, mix and microwave for 6 minutes. Stir once in between.

8   Add tandoori chicken. Cover and microwave for 3 minutes. Remove from oven and let it cool down till serving time.

9   Add milk and microwave for 2 minutes. Add cream and garam masala. Mix and serve hot. Serve hot.

Khumb Matar Miloni

Mushroom and peas in a tomato - yogurt gravy.

Serves 4

INGREDIENTS

1 packet (200 gm) mushrooms (khumb)

1 cup peas (shelled)

2 tbsp oil, 1 tsp ginger-garlic paste

1 tbsp kasoori methi (fenugreek leaves)

PASTE - 1

2 onions, 2 laung (cloves)

seeds of 2 chhoti illaichi (green cardamoms)

1 tsp saunf (fennel)

¼ tsp haldi (turmeric powder)

3 tbsp oil

PASTE - 2

3 tomatoes - cut into 4 pieces

½ cup dahi (yogurt)

1¼ tsp salt, ½ tsp garam masala

½ tsp degi mirch or red chilli powder

METHOD

1   Cut each mushroom into 4 pieces.

2   Put 2 tbsp oil, ginger-garlic paste and mushrooms in a microproof dish. Mix and spread them in the dish. Microwave for 3 minutes. Remove mushrooms from the dish and keep aside.

3   Grind all the ingredients of paste-1 in a mixer to a smooth paste.

4   Grind all the ingredients of paste-2 in a mixer to a smooth paste.

5   For the masala, put the paste-1 of onions in the same microproof dish and microwave for 7 minutes.

6   Add paste-2 of tomatoes and kasoori methi. Mix and microwave for 7 minutes.

7   Add 2 cups water and peas. Microwave for 6 minutes.

8   Add the mushrooms. Microwave for 2 minutes. Serve hot.

Chicken Curry

Simple yet delicious!

Serve 4

INGREDIENTS

500 gm chicken - cut into pieces

¾ cup curd

3 tsp ginger-garlic paste

½ tsp red chilli powder, ½ tsp salt

2 tbsp chopped coriander

PASTE

3 onions, 3 tomatoes

2 laung (cloves), 1 tsp salt

seeds of 1 moti illaichi (black cardamom)

seeds of 2 chhoti illaichi (green cardamom)

4 tbsp oil, 3 tsp coriander (dhania) powder

½ tsp garam masala, ½ tsp degi mirch

METHOD

1. Marinate chicken with curd, ginger garlic paste, red chilli powder, ½ tsp salt and chopped coriander. Keep aside for ½ hour.

2. Grind all ingredients written under paste in a mixer to a smooth paste.

3. In a microproof deep bowl put the prepared onion-tomato paste. Mix well. Microwave for 11 minutes.

4. Add marinated chicken, mix well and microwave covered for 8 minutes.

5. Add 1½ cups of water and microwave covered for 8 minutes.

6. Sprinkle generously with garam masala and serve hot.

Paneer Pista Haryali

You can add anything else also, instead of paneer in this rich green gravy.

Serves 4

INGREDIENTS

200 gm paneer - cut into 1" squares

2 medium sized onions - cut into 4 pieces

¼ cup pistas (pistachio nuts) with the hard cover on - remove
hard cover

½ cup milk

GRIND TOGETHER TO A PASTE

1 green chilli - roughly chopped

¼ cup chopped fresh coriander

1" ginger piece and 4-5 flakes garlic

1 tbsp dhania powder (ground coriander)

½ tsp white pepper powder

¾ tsp salt, or to taste

4 tbsp oil

METHOD

1   Peel and cut each onion into 4 pieces. Put onion pieces and pistas in 1 cup water in a microproof dish and microwave covered for 6 minutes. Cool slightly. Slip the skin of pistas.

2   Grind boiled onion pieces and the pistas along with the water, and with all the other ingredients written under paste to a fine green paste.

3   Put the prepared paste in a microproof dish and microwave for 5 minutes.

4   Add ½ cup water, a small pinch of sugar and paneer and microwave for 2 minutes. Keep aside till serving time.

5   At serving time, add ½ cup milk or slightly more to get a thick gravy. Microwave for 2 minutes. Serve hot.

Chicken Chettinad

The brown fiery curry from South India.

Serves 4-5

INGREDIENTS

½ chicken (400 gm) - cut into 8 small pieces

1 large onion - chopped very finely

¼ cup curry leaves

1 tbsp lemon juice

1 cup milk

PASTE (GRIND TOGETHER)

2 tomatoes

1½" piece ginger, 5 flakes garlic

½ cup freshly grated coconut

½ tsp saboot dhania (coriander seeds)

½ tsp saunf (fennel seeds)

1¼ tsp saboot kali mirch (peppercorns)

3 whole, dry red chillies

2 chhoti illaichi (green cardamoms), 1-2 laung (cloves)

¾ tsp salt, ¼ tsp turmeric powder (haldi)

METHOD

1 Grind together all the ingredients written under paste in a mixer to a very smooth paste with ¼ cup water.

2 Put 3 tbsp oil in a microproof dish, add onion and curry leaves. Microwave for 5 minutes.

3 Add the chicken pieces and microwave covered for 5 minutes.

4 Add the prepared paste and mix and microwave covered for 8 minutes.

5 Add 1¼ cups of water. Microwave covered for 6 minutes. Keep aside.

6 At serving time, add 1 cup milk to the chicken, mix. Check salt and add more if required. Microwave for 3 minutes.

7 Mix well. Add lemon juice to taste. Serve hot garnished with freshly crushed peppercorns.

Ghiya-Channe ki Dal

Split gram lentils cooked with bottle gourd and tempered to perfection.

Serves 4

INGREDIENTS

¾ cup channe ki dal (split gram) - washed & soaked for ½ hour

½ small (200 gms) ghiya (bottle gourd) - peeled & chopped

1 tsp salt

½ tsp haldi (turmeric powder)

2 tsp desi ghee or oil

½ tsp red chilli powder

TOMATO-ONION BAGHAR

3 tbsp oil, 1 tsp cumin seeds (jeera)

1 onion - finely sliced

1 tomato - finely chopped

2 tbsp chopped coriander, 2 green chillies

1 tsp dhania powder

½ tsp garam masala

½ tsp amchoor

½ tsp red chilli powder

METHOD

1 Pick, clean & wash dal. Soak for ½ hour.

2 Drain water from dal. Mix dal, ghiya, salt, haldi, desi ghee, red chilli powder and 2 cups water in a deep bowl. Microwave covered for 6 minutes.

3 Stir once inbetween. Remove cover and microwave for 20 minutes or till dal turns soft. Mash lightly. Cover and keep aside.

4 For the baghar, mix oil with jeera in a microproof dish. Microwave for 2 minutes. Add onions and microwave for 4 minutes till golden.

5 Add tomato, coriander and whole green chillies and all the masalas. Microwave for 3 minutes. Pour over the hot cooked dal. Mix gently. Serve hot.

Makai-Mirch Salan

Baby corn and green chillies in a red gravy flavoured with cumin and mustard seeds.

Serve 4-5

INGREDIENTS

5-6 big green chillies (acchari hari mirch)

200 gm babycorns - keep whole if small or cut into 2 pieces if big

1 tbsp vinegar, 3 tbsp oil

1 tsp jeera (cumin seeds), ½ tsp mustard seeds (rai)

a few curry leaves, 2 onions - chopped finely

2 tsp coriander (dhania) powder

1 tsp salt, ¼ tsp red chilli powder

½ tsp dry mango powder (amchoor)

¼ tsp garam masala

1½ cups readymade tomato puree

1 tsp ginger paste, 3 tbsp roasted peanuts

1 cup water, ¾ cup milk

METHOD

1 Slit the mirch and remove seeds. Sprinkle ½ tsp salt and 1 tbsp vinegar. Rub well and keep aside for 15 minutes. Wash and pat dry on a kitchen towel.

2 Churn peanuts with ¼ cup milk in a mixer to get a paste. Keep aside.

3 In a microproof dish put oil, jeera, rai, curry leaves, chopped onions, dhania powder, salt, red chilli powder, amchoor & garam masala. Mix well. Microwave for 8 minutes.

4 Add mirchi, baby corns, redymade tomato puree and ginger paste. Microwave for 6 minutes.

5 Add prepared peanut paste and 1 cup water. Mix well. Microwave for 5 minutes. Stir well.

6 Add ½ cup milk. Microwave for 1 minute. Serve hot.

Chicken Degi

A bright red chicken curry prepared from Kashmiri mirch.

Serve 5

INGREDIENTS

500 gms chicken - cut into 1" pieces

3 onions - sliced finely (1½ cups)

1½ tsp degi lal mirch powder

½ tsp fennel seeds (saunf) - crushed

6 tbsp oil

4 tomatoes - pureed in a mixer

1 tsp garam masala

1½ tsp salt, or to taste

½ tsp pepper

2 tbsp dry fenugreek leaves (kasoori methi)

seeds of 3 green cardamoms (2 chhoti illaichi)- crushed

2½ cups water

METHOD

1. Put sliced onions, degi mirch, saunf and 3 tbsp oil in a microproof dish. Mix well. Microwave for 10 minutes.

2. Add the pureed tomatoes, garam masala, salt, pepper, kasoori methi and crushed seeds of chhoti illaichi. Mix well. Microwave for 8 minutes.

3. Add chicken and mix very well. Microwave covered for 8 minutes.

4. Add 2½ cups water, microwave covered for 9 minutes. Stir once inbetween. Serve hot.

Pista Murg

Chicken in a pistachio based green gravy.

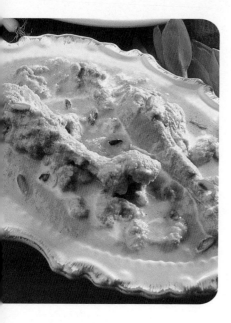

Serves 4

INGREDIENTS

400 gm chciken - cut into 1" pieces

2 medium sized onions - cut into 4 pieces

¼ cup pistas (pistachio nuts) with the hard cover on - remove hard cover

½ cup milk

PASTE (GRIND TOGETHER)

1 green chilli - roughly chopped

¼ cup chopped fresh coriander

1" ginger piece, 4-5 flakes garlic

1 tbsp dhania powder (ground coriander)

½ tsp white pepper powder

¾ tsp salt, or to taste

3 tbsp oil

METHOD

1   Mix 1 tbsp oil and chicken and grill for 8 minutes.

2   Peel & cut each onion into 4 pieces. Put onion pieces and pistas in 1 cup water in a microproof dish and microwave covered for 6 minutes. Cool slightly. Slip the skin of pistas.

3   Grind boiled onion pieces and the green pistas along with the water, and all the other ingredients written under paste and grind to a fine green paste.

4   Put prepared paste in a microproof dish and microwave for 5 minutes.

5   Add ½ cup water, a small pinch of sugar and chicken and microwave for 3 minutes. Keep aside till serving time.

6   At serving time, add ½ cup milk or slightly more to get a thick gravy. Microwave for 2 minutes. Serve hot.

Badami Seekh Curry

Roundels of seekh kebabs in an almond flavoured gravy.

Serve 4

INGREDIENTS

300 gms ready-made seekh kebabs - cut into ½"-¾" thick slices

1 cup milk

1 cup water

ONION PASTE (GRIND TOGETHER)

1 onion

8 flakes of garlic, 1" piece ginger

2 tbsp badam (almonds)

seeds of 2 chhoti illaichi, 2 laung

3 tbsp oil, ¼ tsp jeera (cumin seeds)

OTHER INGREDIENTS

1 tomato - chopped

1 cup ready-made tomato puree

½ tsp Kashmiri laal mirch or degi mirch

pinch of sugar

½ tsp salt, ¼ tsp garam masala

¾ tsp chicken masala

METHOD

1. Put the prepared onion paste in a big microproof dish. Microwave for 4 minutes.

2. Add chopped tomato and the tomato puree, and all the other ingredients. Mix well. Microwave for 6 minutes.

3. Add 1 cup of water, mix well and microwave for 5 minutes.

4. Add milk, mix well and microwave for 2 minutes. Stir. Check salt and keep gravy aside.

5. Mix seekh pieces with 1 tbsp oil. Grill the seekh pieces for 12 minutes, overturning once after 6 minutes.

6. At serving time, add cooked seekh pieces to the gravy. Add more milk if the gravy appears thick. Check salt. Microwave for 2 minutes.

Dum Murg Kali Mirch

Freshly pounded peppercorns lend a subtle spiciness to the dish.

Serves 4

INGREDIENTS

½ of a medium sized chicken (400 gm) - cut into 8 pieces

2-3 chhoti illaichi (green cardamoms)

4 tbsp oil

2 onions - finely chopped

1 tsp saboot kali mirch (peppercorns) - pounded coarsely to a rough powder

½ cup milk

PASTE

5-6 cashewnuts

½ cup thick dahi (yogurt)

½ tsp red chilli powder

1 tsp salt

½ tsp garam masala powder

½" piece of ginger, 10 flakes of garlic

METHOD

1   Grind all the ingredients of paste to a very smooth paste in the mixer.

2   Put oil, chhoti illaichi and the chopped onions in a microproof dish. Mix well and microwave for 8 minutes.

3   Add the chicken pieces and dahi- kaju paste, mix well and microwave covered for 8 minutes.

4   Add ½ cup milk and 1 cup water. Mix. Sprinkle ¾ tsp freshly crushed peppercorns. Microwave for 6 minutes. Stir once inbetween.

5   Sprinkle some crushed peppercorns and serve hot.

Mutton Koftas in Creamy Sauce

Minced meat balls in tomato gravy

Gives 10-12 koftas

INGREDIENTS

KOFTA

500 gm keema (mutton mince)

1 tbsp ginger paste, 1 tbsp garlic paste

3-4 green chillies - chopped finely, 1 tsp garam masala

3 slices bread, 1 egg

1¼ tsp salt, or to taste

¼ cup chopped fresh coriander leaves

GARNISHING

some fresh chopped coriander

CREAMY TOMATO SAUCE

5 large tomatoes, 2½" piece ginger, 1 tsp salt

1 tsp red chilli powder, 1 tsp jeera powder

1 cup malai or cream

a pinch of orange red colour

METHOD

1   To prepare the tomato sauce, blend tomatoes, ginger, salt, chilli powder and jeera in a mixer to a puree.

2   In the dish, add the above tomato puree and microwave covered for 10 minutes.

3   Add cream & a little orange colour. Mix well & keep the creamy tomato sauce aside.

4   To make koftas, soak bread in water, squeeze and crumble.

5   Mix all ingredients of the kofta with the bread. Make into balls.

6   Place balls on a plate in a ring. Microwave uncovered for 5 minutes. Change sides of koftas, inbetween, after 2-3 minutes.

7   Add koftas to the tomato sauce in the dish. Microwave covered for 4 minutes.

8   Let stand for 2-3 minutes. Serve hot garnished with fresh coriander.

Special Sambar

The pulse is blended in a mixer to get a smooth and creamy sambhar.

Serves 4

INGREDIENTS

½ cup arhar dal (red gram dal)

100 gm pumpkin or 2 small brinjals or any other vegetable of your choice - chopped (1 cup)

lemon sized ball of imli (tamarind)

1½ tsp salt or to taste

¼ tsp hing powder (asafoetida)

2 tbsp sambhar powder

1 tbsp oil

1 onion - sliced

½ tsp sarson (mustard seeds)

¼ cup curry leaves

tiny piece of gur (jaggery) - optional

METHOD

1   Put dal in a microproof bowl. Add 1 cup water and microwave covered for 5 minutes. Remove the cover and microwave for 5 more minutes or till dal turns soft. Cool. Add ½ cup water. Mix. Blend in a mixer to a puree.

2   Microwave imli in ½ cup water for 2 minutes. Extract the juice. Add 1 more cup water to the left over imli and mash well. Extract more juice. Keep imli juice aside.

3   Put oil, curry leaves, sarson, sambhar powder and onions in a deep microproof bowl. Mix well. Microwave for 5 minutes.

4   Add the chopped vegetables, salt, pureed dal and imli paani. Cover and microwave for 6 minutes.

5   Add 2 cups water and microwave for 8 minutes. Serve hot.

Khoya Matar

Peas combine with crumbly dried whole milk to give a rich dish.

Serves 4

INGREDIENTS

200 gms khoya - mashed roughly or crumbled

2 cups shelled peas

4 tbsp oil or desi ghee

¾ cup ready made tomato puree

1 tsp red chilli powder, 1 tsp jeera (cumin) powder

¾ tsp garam masala powder

6-8 cashewnuts - split into 2 pieces

1 tsp salt, or to taste

GRIND TOGETHER (ONION PASTE)

2 onions

2 dry, red chillies

1" piece ginger

METHOD

1   In a dish, mix oil and onion paste. Microwave for 8 minutes.

2   Add tomato puree, garam masala, red chilli powder, jeera powder, peas and ¼ cup water. Mix well.

3   Microwave for 4 minutes.

4   Add salt, khoya and ½ cup water. Mix gently to prevent khoya from getting mashed. Sprinkle cashew halves.

5   Microwave for 3 minutes. Serve hot.

Mixed Veggie Curry

Seasonal vegetables in a red tomato based gravy flavoured with cloves and cardamoms.

Serves 4

INGREDIENTS

¼ of a small cauliflower - cut into 8 small (½" florets)

1 carrot - cut into thin round slices

10 french beans - cut into ½" pieces

1 capsicum - cut into ½" cubes

50 gm paneer - cut into ½" cubes

¾ cup ready made tomato puree, 1½ tsp salt, or to taste

1½ cups milk (cold)

GRIND TO A PASTE

2 onions, 2 tbsp ghee or oil

½ " piece ginger, 3-4 flakes garlic

2 laung (cloves) seeds of 1 chhoti illaichi

1 tsp dhania powder

¾ tsp jeera - crushed to a powder

½ tsp garam masala powder

¼-½ tsp red chilli powder

METHOD

1   Cut all the vegetables into ½" pieces. Wash cauliflower, carrots and beans. Microwave together for 3 minutes in a plastic bag or a covered dish. Keep aside.

2   Grind together all ingredients of the   paste. Put onion paste in the dish. Micro uncovered for 8 minutes.

3   Add tomato puree, salt, all microwaved vegetables and capsicum. Mix well.

4   Microwave for 4 minutes.

5   Add paneer and milk. Mix well. Keep aside till serving time.

6   To serve, microwave for 3 minutes.

Water Melon Curry

An unusual thin, spicy curry which is delicious when served with rice.

Serves 4

INGREDIENTS

4 cups of tarbooz (water melon) - cut into 1" pieces along with a little white portion also, and deseeded

4-5 flakes garlic - crushed

½ tsp salt, or to taste

2 tsp lemon juice

2 tbsp oil

½ tsp jeera (cumin seeds)

a pinch of hing (asafoetida)

1 tbsp ginger - cut into thin match sticks

½ tsp dhania (coriander) powder

½ - ¾ tsp red chilli powder

a pinch of haldi (turmeric) powder

GARNISH

chopped green chillies and coriander

METHOD

1 Puree 1½ cups of water melon cubes (the upper soft pieces) with 4-5 flakes of garlic, salt and lemon juice to get about 1 cup of water melon puree. Leave the remaining firm, lower pieces (with the white portion) as it is. Keep aside.

2 Put oil, jeera, hing, ginger, coriander powder, red chilli powder & haldi in a microproof dish. Mix well. Microwave for 2 minutes.

3 Add the remaining water melon pieces or cubes and stir to mix.

4 Add the prepared puree and microwave for 5 minutes. Remove from microwave.

5 Garnish with green chillies and green coriander. Serve hot with boiled rice

Goan Chicken Curry

Chicken in a red Goan curry flavoured with coconut milk and tamarind.

Serve 4

INGREDIENTS

400 gm chicken with bones - cut into pieces

GRIND TO A PASTE

¼ cup chopped or grated coconut

5 dry, red chillies

1 tsp jeera (cumin seeds)

½ tbsp saboot dhania (coriander seeds)

a pinch of haldi (turmeric powder)

1½ tbsp imli (tamarind) - deseeded

1" piece ginger, 5-6 flakes garlic

OTHER INGREDIENTS

2 tbsp oil

1 onion - chopped

1 tomato - chopped

2 cups thin coconut milk

1 tsp salt or to taste

METHOD

1   Mix chicken with 1 tbsp oil. Arrange on the wire rack and grill for 10 minutes. Cool. Debone chicken from its bones into thick long strips. Keep chicken aside.

2   Grind coconut, whole chillies, jeera, saboot dhania, haldi, imli, ginger, garlic and ½ cup water to a paste. Keep coconut paste aside.

3   In a microproof dish put oil and onion. Microwave for 5 minutes.

4   Add chopped tomato and the prepared paste. Mix well. Microwave for 3 minutes.

5   Add coconut powder, milk, water & salt. Mix well. Micro for 6 minutes.

6   Stir well and add grilled chicken. Microwave for 2 minutes. Serve hot.

Murg Lahori

Chicken in a rich white, saffron flavoured gravy.

Serves 4

INGREDIENTS

500 gm chicken with bones - cut into 8 pieces

2 tbsp oil

1 cup curd - hang in a muslin cloth for 15 minutes

1½ tbsp kasoori methi (dried fenugreek leaves)

1 cup milk

¼ tsp saffron (kesar) - soaked in 1 tbsp warm water

PASTE

2 onions

1 green chilli

4 tbsp oil

6 flakes garlic

1½" piece ginger

½ tsp garam masala

1½ tsp salt

1 tsp white pepper (adjust to taste)

METHOD

1   To cook chicken, put the chicken in a bowl. Add oil and mix well. Place on a wire rack. Grill for 10 minutes. Keep chicken aside.

2   Grind together all ingredients of the paste to a smooth paste in a mixer.

3   Put paste in a microproof dish and microwave for 6 minutes.

4   Add hung curd and kasoori methi. Mix very well.

5   Add grilled chicken, 1 cup milk, ½ cup water and soaked kesar. Mix well to coat the chicken with the white masala. Microwave for 3 minutes. Serve hot.

Paneer Makhani

Paneer in a red cashew based makhani gravy flavoured with fenugreek.

Serves 4-5

INGREDIENTS

300 gm paneer - cut into cubes

5 large (500 gm) tomatoes - chopped roughly

1" piece ginger - chopped

2 tbsp butter/ghee and 2 tbsp oil

seeds of 2 green illaichi (cardamoms) - crushed

½ tsp sugar, 1 tsp salt or to taste

½ tsp garam masala

½ tsp degi mirch or red chilli powder

1 tsp tomato ketchup

4 tbsp cashewnuts or magaz - soaked in ¼ cup water and ground to a paste

2 tsp kasoori methi (dried fenugreek leaves)

1 cup milk, approx.

3-4 tbsp cream

METHOD

1   Microwave tomatoes and ginger in a deep dish with ½ cup water for 5 minutes.

2   Blend tomatoes and ginger to a puree in a mixer.

3   Microwave butter/ghee and oil for 2 minutes. Add illaichi powder. Mix. Add salt, sugar, red chilli powder and garam masala. Mix. Add fresh tomato puree and tomato ketchup. Mix very well. Microwave for 8 minutes. Stir once in between.

4   Add cashewnut or magaz paste and kasoori methi. Mix well. Add ½ cup water. Microwave for 3 minutes.

5   Add paneer and mix well. Add enough milk to get a thick red gravy. Mix well and microwave for 3 minutes.

6   Add cream. Sprinkle little kasoori methi on top and serve hot.

Chicken Naveli

Curry powder and coconut milk lend a wonderful flavour to this curry.

Serves 4

INGREDIENTS

400 gms chicken - cut into 6 pieces

½" piece ginger & 3 flakes garlic- crushed to a paste (1 tsp paste)

5 spring onions - sliced diagonally till the greens

4 tbsp oil

1 onion - sliced

3 flakes of garlic - chopped

4 tbsp curry powder (MDH) - mixed with 6 tbsp water

2 cups coconut milk, fresh or readymade

1 tsp salt or to taste

METHOD

1 Crush ginger and garlic to a paste.

2 Diagonally slice spring onions up till the greens.

3 Put oil, sliced onion, chopped garlic, white of spring onions and curry powder in a microproof dish. Microwave for 5 minutes.

4 Add chicken and ginger-garlic paste. Mix well and microwave covered for 8 minutes.

5 Add the coconut milk and 1 tsp salt or to taste. Microwave for 6 minutes.

6 Add the greens of spring onions. Keep aside till serving time.

7 At serving time, microwave for 2 minutes and serve hot with steamed rice.

Corn Korma

The famous curry - "Korma" made quickly in a microwave.

Serves 4

INGREDIENTS

3 tbsp oil

3-4 black cardamoms (moti elaichi)

2 onions - chopped finely

1 tomato - chopped finely

¼ tsp sugar

1 tsp red chilli powder, salt to taste

¼ tsp turmeric (haldi) powder

1 cup yogurt - whisk till smooth

1 cup frozen corn niblets

2 green chillies - deseeded & chopped

¼ tsp garam masala

MASALA PASTE

1 small piece coconut - grated (¼ cup)

2 tsp poppy seeds (khus-khus)

7-8 cashewnuts

GARNISHING

a few coriander leaves - chopped finely

METHOD

1 Grind all the ingredients of the masala paste together to a fine paste, using a little water.

2 Put oil & opened cardamoms in a dish. Micro high 2 minutes uncovered.

3 Add sugar, red chilli powder, salt and turmeric powder. Mix well. Add onions. Micro high 3 minutes.

4 Add masala paste. Mix well. Add tomatoes. Stir well. Micro high covered 5 minutes.

5 Add yogurt, corn, chillies and garam masala. Mix well. Micro high for 7 minutes. Stir once in between.

6 Add ½ cup water. Microwave for 2 minutes. Let it stand for 2 minutes. Sprinkle coriander leaves. Serve.

INDIAN DRY & MASALA

Baigan ka Bharta

Brinjals are easy to cook in a microwave. Not messy at all!

Serves 3-4

INGREDIENTS

1 medium brinjal (350 gm)

2 onions - chopped finely

½ cup ready-made tomato puree

1 tomato - chopped

½" piece ginger - chopped finely

1 green chilli - chopped

2 tsp coriander (dhania) powder

½ tsp garam masala

½ tsp degi mirch or red chilli powder

1 tsp salt

METHOD

1   Place brinjal in a microproof flat dish. Microwave for 5 minutes. Let it cool down. Cut into half and scoop out the pulp. Mash the pulp with a fork and keep pulp aside.

2   In the same dish, put oil, onions, ginger, green chilli, dhania powder, garam masala, degi mirch and microwave for 7 minutes.

3   Add brinjal pulp and cook on combination mode (micro + grill) for 10 minutes.

4   Add chopped tomato and tomato puree and 1 tsp salt. Mix well. Microwave for 6 minutes. Serve hot.

Palak Keema

Capsicums when added instead of the usual peas elevates this common mutton mince recipe.

Serves 4-5

INGREDIENTS

½ kg chicken mince (keema) - wash in a soup strainer

1½ cups spinach (palak)- shredded (cut into thin long strips)

3 tbsp butter

2 onions - chopped

1 tsp jeera (cumin seeds)

½ tsp kalonji (nigella seeds)

¼ tsp methi daana (fenugreek seeds)

½ tsp saunf (fennel seeds) - crushed

1 tbsp chopped coriander - to garnish

TOMATO PASTE (PUREE IN A MIXER)

2 tomatoes

2" piece of ginger

16- 20 flakes of garlic

2-3 dry red chillies, 1¼ tsp salt

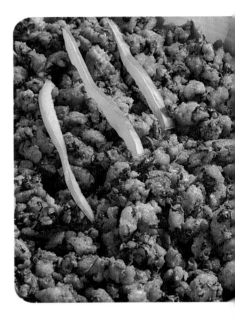

METHOD

1 Put butter in a microproof dish and microwave for 30 seconds.

2 Add jeera, kalonji, methi dana, saunf and chopped onions. Mix well. Microwave for 8 minutes.

3 Add the chicken keema, mix well. Microwave for 7 minutes.

4 Add shredded palak and the prepared tomato paste. Mix and microwave for 7 minutes.

5 Add ¾ cup water, mix and microwave for 5 minutes. Check salt, add more if required.

6 Serve garnished with chopped green coriander.

Murg Kadhai Waala

Chicken in kadhai masala which is flavoured with fenugreek and coriander.

Serves 4-5

INGREDIENTS

1 medium sized (800 gms) chicken - cut into 12 pieces

2 tsp salt, or to taste, 6 tbsp oil

½ tsp methi dana (fenugreek seeds)

3 large onions - cut into slices

15-20 flakes garlic - crushed

4 large tomatoes - chopped

¼ cup ready made tomato puree

½ cup chopped green coriander

1 capsicum - cut into thin long pieces

2" piece ginger - cut into match sticks

1-2 green chillies - cut into thin slices

4-5 tbsp cream

GRIND TOGETHER ROUGHLY

1½ tbsp saboot dhania (coriander seeds)

3 whole, dry red chillies

METHOD

1   Put oil, methi dana and onion slices in a microproof dish and microwave for 10 minutes or till light brown.

2   Add garlic, saboot dhania-red chilli powder and chopped tomatoes and microwave for 6 minutes.

3   Add chicken and salt. Mix very well. Cover and microwave for 11 minutes or till chicken is tender.

4   Add tomato puree, chopped green coriander, capsicum, ginger match sticks and green chilli slices. Mix well. Microwave for 3 minutes

5   Add cream. Mix well and serve hot.

Murg Masala Korma

The typical korma curry made into a semi dry masala which coats the chicken.

Serves 4

INGREDIENTS

½ kg boneless chicken - cut into 1" pieces

2 medium onions - finely sliced

5 tbsp oil

2 tbsp chopped coriander

¾ cup yogurt (dahi) and ¼ cup water - beat together until smooth

ONION PASTE

1 medium sized onion

½" piece of ginger

2-3 flakes of garlic

1 tbsp cashewnuts (kaju)

1 tsp salt or to taste

¼ tsp haldi (turmeric powder)

1 tsp red chilli powder

METHOD

1   Grind all ingredients of the onion paste together to a smooth paste.

2   Put 5 tbsp oil and sliced onions in a microproof dish and microwave for 9 minutes.

3   Add the onion paste and chicken. Mix and microwave for 9 minutes or till chicken gets cooked.

4   Add well beaten curd and microwave for 3 minutes.

5   Add coriander. Mix well. Serve hot.

Crispy Achaari Mirch

Peppers filled with rice with some pickle masala and grilled with a semolina coating till crisp.

Serves 6

INGREDIENTS

125 gms (6) big green chillies (achaari hari mirch) or 3 small capsicums

¼ cup vinegar, ¼ tsp salt

FILLING

1½ cups boiled rice

½ tsp brown mustard seeds (rai)

½ tsp cumin seeds (jeera), ½ tsp fennel seeds (saunf)

1 onion - chopped, ¼ tsp turmeric powder (haldi)

2 tsp of any achaar ka masala (preferably use aam ka achaar)

1 tomato - chopped

½ tsp salt, 1 tsp tomato ketchup

COATING

2 tbsp flour (maida), 4 tbsp semolina (suji)

¼ tsp salt, ¼ tsp garlic paste

METHOD

1   Slit the chillies and remove the seeds. Pour vinegar on them and sprinkle ¼ tsp salt on them. Mix. Keep aside.

2   In a microproof dish put 1 tbsp oil, jeera, rai, saunf, chopped onion, and haldi. Mix well. Microwave for 5 minutes.

3   Add boiled rice, aam ke aachar ka masala, ½ tsp salt, chopped tomato and tomato ketchup. Mix well.

4   Fill each mirchi with the filling. Fill as much as the mirchi can take.

5   Mix ingredients of coating in a plate.

6   Put 2-3 tbsp oil in a bowl. Dip the sides of the mirchi in the oil and then immediately roll over the coating spread in the plate. Coat all the sides of the mirchi with the coating mixture nicely.

7   Grill for 12-15 minutes or till golden. Serve hot.

Tikka Masala

Chicken tikka converted into a meal time dish.

Serves 4

INGREDIENTS

½ kg cooked chicken tikka - (prepare chicken tikka as given on page 14)

MASALA

4 tomatoes

5 tbsp oil, ½ tsp sarson (mustard seeds)

½ tsp kalonji (onion seeds) or jeera (cumin seeds)

2 onions - sliced, 3-4 flakes of garlic- crushed

4 green chillies - finely chopped

1 cup coconut milk

4 tbsp mint (poodina) leaves - chopped

4 tbsp coriander - finely chopped

3 tbsp lemon juice

1 tsp salt, 1 tsp garam masala

METHOD

1   Prepare chicken tikka as given on page 14.

2   Place tomatoes in a microproof dish and microwave for 3 minutes. Peel the skin of the tomatoes and chop finely.

3   Put oil, sarson, kalonji or jeera, sliced onions, crushed garlic, chopped green chillies and tomatoes. Mix well. Microwave for 7 minutes.

4   Add coconut milk and microwave for 4 minutes. Keep aside till serving time.

5   At serving time, add cooked chicken tikka, chopped mint, coriander, lemon juice, garam masala and salt to the masala in the dish. Mix. Microwave for 2 minutes.

Chicken Bharta

Dices of chicken cooked in onion - tomato masala.

Serves 4

INGREDIENTS

500 gms boneless chicken - cut into tiny pieces

3 onions - chopped

1 tbsp saboot dhania - crushed

1½" piece ginger- chopped

10 flakes garlic - chopped

3 tomatoes - chopped

1 big tomato - pureed in a mixer

2 dry, red chillies - break into pieces

1½ tsp salt

1 tsp garam masala

1 tsp coriander (dhania) powder

½ tsp dry mango powder (amchoor)

2 tbsp kasoori methi (dry fenugreek leaves)

2 green chillies - keep whole, do not chop

2 tbsp chopped coriander

METHOD

1   Cut boneless chicken into thin long strips & cut each of this strip into small pieces.

2   Put 4 tbsp oil, chopped onion, crushed saboot dhania, ginger and garlic in a microproof dish and microwave for 9 minutes.

3   Add chicken, mix well and microwave covered for 4 minutes.

4   Add chopped tomatoes, pureed tomatoes, dry red chillies, salt, garam masala, dhania powder, amchoor, kasoori methi and whole green chillies. Mix well. Cook on combination mode (micro+grill) for 10 minutes. Stir once in between.

5   Garnish with fresh coriander and serve hot.

Paneer Hara Pyaz

Green spring onions with cottage cheese in masala.

Serves 4

INGREDIENTS

250 gm paneer- cut into 1" cubes

150 gm hare pyaz (spring onions)

1 green chilli - deseeded & chopped

3 tbsp oil

6-8 flakes garlic - crushed

¼ tsp turmeric powder (haldi)

2 tsp coriander (dhania) powder

¾ cup readymade tomato puree

1 tbsp tomato ketchup

3 laung (cloves) - crushed

½ tsp red chilli powder

½ tsp garam masala

¾ tsp salt

4 tbsp cream or well beaten thin malai

METHOD

1   Cut white of spring onions into rings, greens into ½" diagonal pieces.

2   Put oil, garlic, white of onion, haldi and dhania powder in a microproof dish. Microwave for 4 minutes.

3   Add tomato puree, tomato ketchup, laung, red chilli powder, garam masala and salt. Mix well. Microwave for 4 minutes.

4   Add ½ cup water, paneer, green chillies, cream and about 1 cup of greens of spring onions. Mix well. Microwave for 2 minutes. Check salt and add more if required. Mix and serve hot.

Anjeeri Gobhi

Cauliflower cooked with a hint of sweetness in a yogurt and dry figs paste.

Serves 4-6

INGREDIENTS

½ kg (1 big) cauliflower (gobhi) - cut into medium size florets with long stalks

1 tsp jeera (cumin seeds)

2 onions - chopped

¾" piece ginger - chopped

¼ tsp turmeric (haldi)

2 green chillies

1 tomato - chopped

ANJEER PASTE

8 small anjeers (figs) - chopped

¾ cup dahi (yogurt)

½ tsp garam masala

½ tsp red chilli powder

1½ tsp salt

METHOD

1   Break the cauliflower into medium florets, keeping the stalk intact.

2   Churn all the ingredients given under anjeer paste in a mixer till smooth.

3   In a microproof dish put 4 tbsp oil, jeera, chopped onions and ginger. Add haldi. Mix. Microwave for 9 minutes.

4   Add the prepared anjeer paste. Mix well. Add cauliflower and mix very well. Mix in whole green chillies and chopped tomato. Cover and microwave for 10 minutes or more till the cauliflower gets cooked.

Achaari Bhindi

Crispy fried ladys fingers with pickle spices.

Serves 4

INGREDIENTS

500 gm bhindi (lady's finger)

1 tsp ginger paste

½ tsp red chilli powder

1 tsp dhania powder

½ tsp amchoor

½ tsp garam masala

¾ tsp salt, or to taste

2 big tomatoes - chopped

1 tsp lemon juice

ACHAARI SPICES

a pinch of hing (asafoetida)

1 tsp saunf (fennel)

½ tsp rai (mustard seeds)

½ tsp kalonji (onion seeds)

METHOD

1   Wash bhindi and wipe dry. Cut the tip of the head of each bhindi, leaving the pointed end as it is. Now cut the bhindi vertically from the middle making 2 smaller pieces from each bhindi.

2   Keep bhindi in a dish. Sprinkle 2 tbsp oil on it. Mix well. Put them in the oven on combination mode (micro+grill) for 15 minutes or till cooked and crisp. Keep aside.

3   In the separate small dish put 2 tbsp oil and achari spices. Microwave for 3 minutes.

4   To the bhindi, add achari spices, dry masala powders, salt, ginger paste, tomatoes and lemon juice. Mix very well. Microwave for 4 minutes. Serve hot.

Dal Maharani

Split and dehusked black lentils cooked till each grain stands out separately.

Serve 4

INGREDIENTS

1 cup dhuli urad dal (split black beans) - soaked for 1 hour

1 onion - sliced

1" piece ginger - grated

3 tbsp oil

1¼ tsp salt

½ tsp turmeric powder (haldi)

½ tsp red chilli powder

¼ tsp amchoor

¼ tsp coriander (dhania) powder

METHOD

1   Clean and wash dal. Soak in water for 1 hour.

2   Keep onion and ginger in a microproof dish. Sprinkle oil on it. Mix. Add salt, haldi, chilli powder, amchoor and dhania powder. Microwave for 6 minutes.

3   Drain the dal and add dal to the onions. Add 2 cups water. Mix well. Microwave covered for 20 minutes. Stir once after 8 minutes in-between.

4   After it is ready, let it stand for 3-4 minutes till it turns soft. Sprinkle chopped coriander and mix gently with a fork.

Murg Amravati

Chicken cooked with a predominant flavour of coconut and peanuts.

Serves 4

INGREDIENTS

500 gm chicken with bones

2 onions - grated, 2 onions - sliced

4 tbsp oil

2 tsp mustard seeds (sarson)

2 tbsp roasted peanuts (moongphali)

4 tbsp grated fresh coconut

½ tsp turmeric powder (haldi)

1½ tsp salt, or to taste

4 tbsp tomato puree (ready-made)

3 tbsp lemon juice

PASTE

2 dry chillies, 1" piece of ginger

2 tbsp cashewnuts (kaju)

2 tsp coriander (dhania) powder

2 cloves (laung), 6 peppercorns (saboot kali mirch)

2 tbsp curd (yogurt)

a pinch of nutmeg (jaiphal)

METHOD

1   Grind all the ingredients of the paste together in a mixer. Keep aside.

2   In a microproof bowl add oil, mustard seeds, sliced and grated onion. Mix well. Microwave for 10 minutes.

3   Add chicken and the prepared paste. Mix. Microwave covered for 8 minutes.

4   Add peanuts, grated coconut, haldi and salt and grill for 5 minutes.

5   Add readymade tomato puree. Mix well and microwave for 4 minutes.

6   Add lemon juice, mix and serve hot.

Chicken Haldighati

Whole coriander seeds and peppercorns combined deliciously with chicken.

Serve 4

INGREDIENTS

½ kg chicken with bones - cut into 6 pieces

5 onions - cut into fine rings (circles)

1 tsp lemon juice, 5 tbsp oil

½ cup milk

½ cup cream or well beaten malai

1½ tbsp chopped coriander

WET PASTE

1 cup dahi (curd), 2 green chillies, 1" piece ginger

1½ tsp saboot dhania (coriander seeds)

1 tsp jeera (cumin seeds)

6 saboot kali mirch (pepper corns)

4 laung (cloves), 1 tsp haldi (turmeric powder)

¾ tsp coriander (dhania) powder

½ tsp garam masala

½ tsp red chilli powder

1½ tsp salt or to taste

METHOD

1   Grind all ingredients of the wet paste together in a mixer to a paste.

2   Put oil and onion rings in a microproof dish. Mix. Microwave for 10 minutes.

3   Add chicken, mix. Microwave covered for 8 minutes.

4   Add the prepared ground wet paste and chopped coriander. Mix well. Microwave for 5 minutes.

5   Add milk and cream or malai. Mix and microwave for 2 minutes.

6   Remove from microwave. Sprinkle lemon juice. Serve hot.

Bharwan Baingan

Brinjals stuffed with a crunchy sesame filling.

Serves 4

INGREDIENTS

8 (300 gm) small brinjals (baingans)

3 tbsp oil

½ tsp cumin seeds (jeera)

1 onion - grated

1½ tsp ginger-garlic paste

¼ tsp each of - sugar, salt, garam masala and red chilli powder

1 tsp full tamarind (imli)

STUFFING (MIX TOGETHER)

2 tbsp roasted peanuts - crushed roughly

2 tsp sesame seeds (til)

1 tsp salt, ½ tsp amchoor

½ tsp haldi, ½ tsp sugar

½ tsp red chilli powder

½ tsp garam masala

2 tsp dhania powder

2 tsp oil

METHOD

1   Put imli with ½ cup water in a small bowl. Microwave for 1 minute. Let it cool. Mash and extract juice and keep aside

2   Wash and slit brinjals, making cross cuts, a little more than half way.

3   Mix all ingredients of the stuffing nicely. Fill the paste in the baingans.

4   Arrange brinjals in a dish. Pour 2 tbsp oil on them. Microwave covered for 8 minutes. Remove from dish and keep aside.

5   In the same dish put 1 tbsp oil, jeera, onion and ginger-garlic paste. Mix well and microwave for 4 min.

6   Add tamarind juice, ¼ tsp of sugar, salt, garam masala and red chilli powder. Mix well. Add cooked brinjals and mix gently for the masala to coat. Microwave covered for 2 minutes. Serve hot.

Mili-Juli-Subzi

Mixed vegetables flavoured with cardamoms.

Serves 4

INGREDIENTS

1 big potato

200 gm (1 packet of 15- 20 pieces) baby cabbage (brussel sprouts) - trim the stalk end or use ½ of a small cabbage - cut into 1" pieces

100 gms baby corns (7-8) - keep whole

½ cup peas (matar)

1 carrot - cut into ¼" pieces (½ cup)

8-10 french beans - cut into ½" pieces

15 cherry tomatoes or 2 regular tomatoes - cut into 4, remove pulp

ONION PASTE (GRIND TOGETHER)

1 onion, 2 cloves (laung)

seeds of 2 green cardamoms (illaichi)

TOMATO PASTE (GRIND TOGETHER)

2 tomatoes

¼ cup curd

¼ tsp haldi, 1 tsp salt, ½ tsp chilli pd

½ tsp garam masala, ½ tsp degi mirch

METHOD

1   Peel potatoes and make balls with the help of a melon scooper.

2   Put 1 cup of water, 2 tsp salt, potato balls in a deep bowl & microwave for 5 minutes.

3   To the same water add cabbage, baby corns, peas, carrots and french beans. Microwave covered for 2 minutes. Strain.

4   Put 3 tbsp oil & onion paste in a microproof bowl. Microwave for 5 minutes.

5   Add tomato paste. Mix. Microwave for 7 minutes.

6   Add ½ cup water and vegetables. Mix well. Microwave covered for 3 minutes. Serve hot.

Murg Jalfrezi

Boneless chicken strips lightly coated with a tomato masala.

Serves 4

INGREDIENTS

½ kg boneless chicken - cut into thin long strips

2 tbsp oil

1 capsicum - cut into strips

¼ cup cream or malai

PASTE (GRIND TOGETHER)

6 flakes garlic

1½" piece ginger

3 tomatoes

1 tbsp tomato sauce

1 tsp salt

½ tsp garam masala

½ tsp jeera (cumin) powder

½ tsp red chilli powder

¼ tsp haldi

1 tsp coriander (dhania) powder

¼ tsp pepper (optional)

3 tbsp oil

METHOD

1   Grind together all the ingredients written under paste to a smooth paste in a mixer.

2   In a microproof deep dish add the chicken and oil. Microwave covered for 6 minutes.

3   Add the prepared tomato paste. Mix well. Microwave covered for 8 minutes.

4   Add cream and capsicum. Mix. Microwave for 3 minutes.

5   Garnish with chopped coriander leaves and garam masala. Serve hot.

Grilled Besani Subzi

Gramflour and carom seeds on top of mixed vegetables give a fragrant roasted flavour when grilled.

Serves 4

INGREDIENTS

2 carrots - cut into thin round slices

2 capsicums - sliced into thin fingers

75 gm paneer - cut into thin fingers (¾ cup)

3 tbsp oil

½ tsp ajwain (carom seeds)

3 tbsp besan (gramflour)

1 tsp lemon juice

¼ tsp red chilli powder

¼ tsp dhania powder

¼ tsp haldi

2 tsp channa masala

2 tsp amchoor

1 tbsp milk

1 tsp salt

1 tomato - deseeded & cut into thin fingers

METHOD

1   Microwave sliced carrots with ¼ cup water in a microproof dish for 3 minutes.

2   In another microproof dish put oil, ajwain, besan, lemon juice, red chilli powder, dhania powder, haldi, channa masala and amchoor. Mix & microwave for 2 minutes.

3   Add carrot, capsicum, paneer, milk and salt.

4   Grill in the oven for 16 minutes. After 8 minutes, add deseeded tomatoes and mix gently with a fork and grill for the remaining 8 minutes. Serve hot.

Mutton Keema

Capsicums when added instead of the usual peas elevates this common mutton mince recipe.

Serves 3-4

INGREDIENTS

250 gm mutton mince (keema)

2 capsicums - chopped

2 tomatoes - chopped, 2 tomatoes - pureed in a mixer

2 tbsp dry fenugreek leaves (kasoori methi)

1 tsp salt

¾ tsp garam masala

¾ tsp roasted jeera powder

2 onions - chopped

1 clove (laung), seeds of 1 black cardamom

1 tsp chopped ginger, 1 tsp chopped garlic

1 green chilli - chopped

½ tsp garam masala

½ tsp red chilli powder

½ tsp coriander (dhania) powder

2 tbsp oil

METHOD

1 In a microproof dish add 2 tbsp oil, onion, laung, moti illiachi, ginger, chopped garlic, green chilli, garam masala, red chilli powder and dhania powder. Microwave for 7 minutes.

2 Add keema and cook on combination mode (micro+grill) for 12 minutes.

3 Add pureed tomatoes, chopped tomatoes, chopped capsicum, kasoori methi, salt and ¼ cup water. Mix. Microwave for 6 minutes.

4 Sprinkle ¾ tsp garam masala and ¾ tsp roasted jeera. Serve hot.

RICE

Coconut Murg Pulao

Whole spices, dried red chillies and coconut milk make this rice very fragrant and spicy.

Serves 4

INGREDIENTS

2 cups basmati rice - soaked for 30 minutes in water

500 gms chicken, with or without bones - cut into 6 small pieces

7 tbsp oil

3 tsp salt, 1 tsp haldi powder

4½ cups ready-made coconut milk

3½ tbsp lemon juice

PASTE (makes ½ cup approx.)

10 dried, red chillies, 2 onions - chopped

12-14 flakes garlic, 4 tsp chopped ginger

2 tbsp cumin seeds (jeera), 2 tsp saunf (fennel)

2" stick dalchini (cinnamon)

seeds of 4 moti illaichi (cardamom)

¼ tsp grated jaiphal (nutmeg)

4 tbsp saboot dhania (coriander seeds)

4 laung (cloves)

8 saboot kali mirch (black peppercorns)

METHOD

1   For the paste grind all ingredients to a fine paste. Use little water if needed.

2   Put chicken, oil and the prepared paste in a big microproof dish. Cover and microwave for 10 minutes.

3   Drain rice. Add salt, haldi, coconut milk and the soaked rice. Mix well gently.

4   Cover and microwave for 8 minutes.

5   Sprinkle lemon juice, mix gently with a fork. Cover and microwave for 7 minutes.

6   Separate the grains with a fork. Serve after 5 minutes, garnished with lemon wedges and tomato slices.

Subz Pulao

The spice bag added to rice while being cooked with the vegetables, makes it very aromatic.

Serves 4

INGREDIENTS

1 cup basmati rice - washed and soaked

5 tbsp oil

1 tsp ginger paste, ½ tsp garlic paste

¼ tsp haldi, ½ tsp red chilli powder, 1½ tsp salt or to taste

SABOOT MASALA OR SPICE BAG (crush together & tie in a piece of muslin cloth)

10 saboot kali mirch (pepper corns)

2 tsp saunf (fennel seeds)

3-4 chhoti illaichi (green cardamom)

3-4 moti illaichi (black cardamom)

4 laung (cloves), 2 sticks dalchini (cinnamon)

VEGETABLES

1 potato - cut into ½" pieces

½ of a small cauliflower - cut into florets

2 carrots - cut into ½" pieces, 1 cup green peas

1 tomato - cut into 8 pieces

2-3 green chillies - cut into thin strips

1 tbsp mint leaves, 1 tsp lemon juice

METHOD

1   In a broad microproof dish, put oil, ginger, garlic, cauliflower, potato, carrots and peas. Microwave for 3 minutes.

2   Drain the soaked rice. Add rice, 2 cups water, haldi, red chilli pd and salt. Add the spice bag. Microwave covered for 6 minutes.

3   Add tomatoes, mint, coriander, green chillies and lemon juice. Stir gently with a fork. Cover and microwave for 7 minutes. Wait for 5 minutes. Fluff with a fork. Remove spice bag. Serve.

CHINESE AND THAI

Honey Chilli Veggies

Sweet and spicy mixed vegetables with Chinese sauces.

Serves 4

INGREDIENTS

1 large carrot, 8-10 mushrooms - keep whole

4-5 baby corns - divide into two lengthwise

1½ cups cauliflower or broccoli - cut into small, flat florets

1 onion - cut into 8 pieces

1 capsicum - cut into ½" cubes

4 tbsp oil

2-3 dry, red chillies - broken into bits & deseeded

15 flakes garlic - crushed

¾ tsp salt and ¼ tsp pepper, or to taste

a pinch ajinomoto (optional)

1½ tbsp vinegar, 1 tsp soya sauce

2½ tbsp tomato ketchup, 2-3 tsp red chilli sauce

3-4 tsp honey, according to taste

3 tbsp cornflour dissolved in ½ cup water along with 1 soup cube

METHOD

1   Dissolve cornflour in ½ cup water. Add soup cube and keep aside.

2   Put oil, broken red chillies, garlic, baby corns, mushrooms, carrots, cauliflower and onion in a microproof dish. Mix well. Microwave for 5 minutes.

3   Add pepper, salt, ajinomoto, chilli sauce, tomato sauce, soya sauce, honey and vinegar. Mix and microwave for 1 minute.

4   Add capsicum and dissolved cornflour and mix. Microwave for 3 minutes or till the vegetables are crisp-tender and the sauce coats the veggies. Mix well before serving. Serve hot with rice or noodles.

Chicken in Hot Garlic Sauce

Enjoy this common Chinese dish with fried rice or noodles.

Serves 4

INGREDIENTS

250 gms chicken breast boneless

4 tbsp oil

2 tbsp chopped & crushed garlic

2 dry, red chillies - broken into pieces

3 tbsp tomato ketchup

3 tsp red chilli sauce

2 tsp soya sauce

1 capsicum - cut into tiny cubes

1 big spring onion - chopped with the greens

½ tsp pepper, 1 tsp salt, a pinch sugar

¼ tsp ajinomoto (optional)

1½ cups water

1 chicken soup cube

2 tsp vinegar

3 tbsp cornflour

METHOD

1   Cut chicken breast into ½" pieces.

2   Put the chicken with 1 tbsp oil, in a microproof bowl. Mix well and microwave covered for 3 minutes. Remove from dish and keep aside.

3   Put 4 tbsp oil, garlic, dry red chilli pieces and white of onion in a microproof dish. Mix and microwave for 3 minutes.

4   Add ketchup, chilli sauce, soya sauce, pepper, sugar, ajinomoto, 2 cups water, crushed soup cube, vinegar & cornflour. Mix well. Microwave for 6   minutes. Stir once in between.

5   Add the cooked chicken, greens of spring onion and capsicum. Mix and microwave covered for 3 minutes or till the sauce turns thick. Check salt and add more if required. Stir well and serve hot.

Paneer in Hot Garlic Sauce

Cottage cheese can be substituted with tofu if available.

Serve 3-4

INGREDIENTS

200 gm paneer

1 capsicum - cut into tiny cubes

3 tbsp oil

20 flakes garlic - crushed (1½ tbsp)

2 dry, red chillies - broken into pieces

4 tbsp tomato ketchup

2 tsp red chilli sauce

2 tsp Soya sauce

½ tsp pepper, 1 tsp salt

a pinch sugar, 2 tsp vinegar

¼ tsp ajinomoto (optional)

1½ cups water

2 tbsp cornflour mixed with ½ cup water

METHOD

1   Put oil, garlic, red chilli pieces, tomato ketchup, red chilli sauce, soya sauce, pepper and ajinomoto in a microproof dish. Mix well, microwave for 2 minutes.

2   Add water, salt, sugar and vinegar. Mix and microwave for 6 minutes.

3   Add cornflour paste, microwave for 3 minutes or more till slightly thick. Mix.

4   Cut paneer into 1" cubes.

5   At serving time, add paneer and capsicum to the sauce and microwave for 2 minutes. Mix well before serving. Serve with noodles or rice.

Thai Green Curry

Chicken in a spicy green curry prepared from green chillies, spring onions and coconut milk.

Serves 5-6

INGREDIENTS

½ kg chicken (500 gms) - cut into ½" pieces, 2 tbsp oil

a tiny piece of gur (jaggery) or 1½ tsp shakkar

2 cups readymade coconut milk

GREEN CURRY PASTE

12 green chillies - deseed if you like a mild curry

1 lemon grass stalks - chopped

½" piece ginger, ½ onion - chopped, 4 flakes garlic

¼ cup chopped coriander leaves & stalk

¼ cup chopped fresh basil leaves

1 tsp salt, ¼ tsp grated nutmeg (jaiphal), 2 tbsp oil

ROAST TOGETHER AND GRIND

1 tsp cumin seeds (jeera)

1 tsp peppercorns (saboot kali mirch)

1 tsp fennel, 2 tsp coriander seeds (saboot dhania)

METHOD

1   Prepare green curry paste by roasting dry spices for 2 minutes. Grind to a powder. Add everything given under the green paste in the grinder along with the spices and add about ¾ cup water. Grind to a fine paste.

2   In a microproof dish add, green paste and oil. Mix well. Microwave uncovered for 2 minutes.

3   Add chicken. Mix well. Microwave covered for 4 minutes.

4   Add jaggery & coconut milk. Mix well so that jaggery dissolves. Microwave uncovered for 6 minutes.

5   Let it stand for 2-3 minutes. Check salt content and the doneness of chicken. If not done, microwave for 1-2 minutes more.

6   Serve garnished with chopped red chillies or coriander or basil leaves.

Dry Chilli Chicken

Succulent pieces of chicken in a spicy Chinese flavouring.

Serve 3-4

INGREDIENTS

350 gm chicken - cut into ½" pieces

½ onion - cut into slices, ½" piece ginger - chopped fine

2-3 flakes garlic - chopped fine, 2 tbsp soya sauce

½ tsp ajinomoto (optional), 1 tbsp vinegar

4-5 green chillies - slit lengthwise

1 medium capsicum - cut into thin strips

1 tsp sugar, 1 tsp salt

2 tsp sherry or white wine (optional)

1½ tbsp cornflour mixed with ½ cup water

METHOD

1   In a microproof dish add 3 tbsp oil, onion, ginger, garlic, soya sauce, ajinomoto and chicken pieces. Mix. Microwave covered for 5 minutes.

2   Add all remaining ingredients. Mix. Microwave uncovered for 3 minutes. Mix and serve hot.

Carrot Pepper Rice

Serve 2-3

INGREDIENTS

1 cup rice - soaked for 15-20 minutes

3 tbsp oil, 1 onion - sliced

1 capsicum & 1 carrot - chopped

1 tsp salt, ½ tsp freshly crushed pepper

½ tsp soya sauce

METHOD

1   Mix oil, onion, capsicum, carrot in a big microproof dish & microwave for 3 minutes.

2   Add rice, 2 cups water, salt, pepper and soya sauce. Microwave covered for 13 minutes. Stir once in between. Sprinkle pepper. Serve after 5 minutes.

Stir Fried Schezwan Chicken

Spicy chicken topped with spring onion greens.

Serve 5-6

INGREDIENTS

500 gm chicken - cut into 1" pieces

10 dry, red chillies

3 tbsp oil

1 tbsp garlic paste

1 tbsp (8- 10 flakes) garlic - chopped fine

5 tbsp tomato ketchup

1 tbsp vinegar, 2 tbsp red chilli sauce

2 tbsp soya sauce, 1 tsp sugar

1-½ tsp red chilli powder

a little red colour (optional)

¼ tsp ajinomoto (optional)

ADD LATER

2 spring onions - cut into 1" diagonal pieces upto the greens

1 tsp salt

2 tbsp (level) cornflour

METHOD

1   In the microproof dish, mix together oil, chopped garlic, dry red chillies, chicken, garlic paste and all the ingredients except spring onions, salt and cornflour. Mix well. Microwave covered for 8 minutes.

2   Add spring onions, salt and cornflour dissolved in ½ cup water. Mix well. Microwave uncovered for 3 minutes or more till a thick sauce coats the chicken. Stir once in between.

3   Let it stand for 2 minutes. Serve hot.

Veggie Thai Red Curry

Mixed vegetables in a lemon flavoured, spicy red curry prepared from coconut milk.

Serves 4-6

INGREDIENTS

RED CURRY PASTE

4-5 dry, Kashmiri red chillies - soaked in ½ cup warm water for 10 minutes

½ onion - chopped

8-10 flakes garlic - peeled, 1½" piece ginger - chopped

1 stalk lemon grass or rind of 1 lemon

1½ tsp coriander seeds (dhania saboot)

1 tsp cumin seeds (jeera), 6 peppercorns (saboot kali mirch)

1 tsp salt, 1 tbsp vinegar

VEGETABLES

7-8 baby corns - slit lengthwise

2 small brinjals - peeled and diced

1 small broccoli or ½ cauliflower - cut into small florets

7-8 mushrooms - sliced

OTHER INGREDIENTS

2½ cups ready made coconut milk

½ tsp soya sauce, 2 tbsp chopped basil or coriander

salt to taste, ½ tsp brown sugar

METHOD

1   Grind all the ingredients of paste with the water in which the chillies were soaked, to a very fine red paste.

2   Mix 2 tbsp oil & red paste in a microproof dish. Microwave for 3 minutes.

3   Add ½ cup of coconut milk, vegetables and microwave for 4 minutes.

4   Add the rest of the coconut milk, soya sauce and chopped basil. Mix and microwave for 4 minutes.

5   Add salt and sugar to taste. Microwave for 1 minute. Serve hot with steamed rice.

CONTINENTAL & BAKED DISHES

Vegetable au Gratin

Mixed vegetables baked in a cheese sauce topped with bread crumbs and tomato slices.

Serve 8

INGREDIENTS

WHITE SAUCE

4 tbsp butter, 4 tbsp maida (plain flour)

2½ cups milk, salt, pepper to taste, 1 tbsp tomato ketchup

VEGETABLES

10-15 french beans - cut into ¼" pieces

2 carrots - cut into small cubes

½ small cauliflower - cut into ½" florets, ½ cup shelled peas

1 medium potato - cut into small cubes

½ of small ghiya (bottle gourd) - peeled & cut into small cubes (1 cup)

TOPPING

¼ cup bread crumbs, 1 tomato - sliced

METHOD

1   To prepare the sauce, melt butter for 50 seconds in a microproof dish.

2   Add flour, salt, pepper, tomato ketchup. Microwave for 30 seconds.

3   Add milk. Mix well. Microwave for 6 minus. Keep sauce aside.

4   Wash vegetables and put in a microproof deep bowl with 1 tsp salt and ¼ cup water. Microwave covered for 5 minutes.

5   Mix vegetables with the prepared sauce. Add salt if required. Microwave for 3 minutes or till sauce turns thick and coats the vegetables.

6   Arrange tomato slices over it. Sprinkle bread crumbs.

7   Set microwave oven at 200°C using the oven (convection) mode and press start to preheat oven. Put the vegetables inside the hot oven and set the preheated oven for 30 minutes. Bake till golden brown. Serve hot.

Stuffed Tomatoes

Tomatoes stuffed with cottage cheese mixed with some tomato ketchup and chilli sauce.

Serve 6-8

INGREDIENTS

6 medium sized tomatoes

100 gm cottage cheese (paneer) - mashed roughly (1 cup)

50 gm grated cheese (½ cup)

½ cup onion - chopped fine

½ cup boiled peas or corn

2 tbsp tomato ketchup

2 tbsp chilli sauce

½ tsp salt

½ tsp garam masala

1 tsp amchoor (dried mango powder)

GARNISH

a few coriander leaves

METHOD

1 Cut tomatoes into 2 halves. Remove pulp and keep inverted for 3-4 minutes.

2 Mix all other ingredients gently in a bowl, taking care not to mash the paneer.

3 Spoon filling into tomato halves and arrange in a ring on a microproof plate. Microwave at combi mode (micro+grill) for 5 minutes.

4 Allow to stand for 2 minutes. Serve hot garnished with coriander leaves.

Chicken Potato Pie

Chicken topped with mashed potatoes and baked till potatoes turn golden.

Serves 2-3

INGREDIENTS

250 gm boneless chicken pieces - cut into ½" pieces

4 tbsp butter

½ packet ready made vegetable soup

2 cups boiled and grated potatoes (4)

1 tsp salt

½ tsp pepper

½ cup grated cheese (50 gm)

2 tbsp chopped parsley or coriander

¼ tsp peppercorns - crushed

METHOD

1   Melt butter for 50 seconds in a microproof dish.

2   Add the chicken pieces and microwave covered for 4 minutes. Add ¼ tsp salt and ¼ tsp pepper. Mix. Remove chicken from the microwave and keep aside.

3   Dissolve ½ packet of soup in 1¼ cups of water in a bowl. Microwave for 6 minutes. Add ¼ tsp salt and ¼ tsp pepper or to taste.

4   Place the chicken pieces in a greased glass baking dish and pour the soup.

5   To the mashed potatoes add 3 tbsp butter, ¼ tsp salt and ¼ tsp pepper. Mix well. Lay the potato mixture over the chicken. Mark it with a fork.

6   Sprinkle cheese, coriander & pepper.

7   Set your microwave oven at 200°C using the oven (convection) mode to preheat.

8   Put the pie inside the hot oven. Set the preheated oven for 20 minutes. Cook till potatoes turn golden from the top.

Rice-Vegetable Ring

Saucy vegetables surrounded by a ring of rice mixed with green herbs.

Serves 5-6

INGREDIENTS

RICE (MIX TOGETHER)

2 cups cooked rice

¼ cup chopped parsley or coriander

salt and lemon juice to taste

OTHER INGREDIENTS

2 tbsp butter

100 gm baby corns - sliced

2 cups finely chopped spinach

2½ tbsp flour (maida), 2 cups milk

¾ tsp salt, 1 tsp pepper, 1½ tsp oregano

1½ cup grated mozzarella cheese

2 tbsp bread crumbs

some tomato slices & black olives

METHOD

1   Melt butter in a microproof dish for 40 seconds.

2   Add oregano, spinach & baby corns Microwave uncovered for 5 minutes.

3   Add flour. Mix well and microwave uncovered for 1 minute.

4   Add milk, salt, 2 tbsp cheese and pepper. Mix. Microwave uncovered for 5 minutes. Keep vegetables aside.

5   Spread parsley rice in a greased dish. Push rice toward the edges of the dish to get a rice border. Sprinkle ½ cup cheese on it. Leaving aside the border of rice put the vegetables in the center portion of the dish, such that the rice border forms a ring around the vegetables. Sprinkle bread crumbs. Arrange tomato slices and sprinkle the left over grated cheese. Sprinkle olives. Dot with butter.

6   To serve, microwave for 4 minutes.

Macaroni Alfredo

Macaroni with vegetables cooked in cheese sauce. Tastes even better if grilled till golden brown.

Serves 5-6

INGREDIENTS

1 cup uncooked macaroni

100 gm mushrooms - sliced

50-100 gm baby corns - sliced (optional)

2 tbsp butter

1 tsp oregano

1 onion or 2 spring onions - chopped along with the green parts

2½ tbsp flour (maida)

1¾ cups milk

¾ tsp salt, or to taste

½ tsp pepper, ½ tsp red chilli flakes

100 gm mozerrela cheese - grated

¼ cup cream, some tomato slices & chopped parsely

METHOD

1   Put 1½ cups of water and 1 tsp oil in a deep microproof bowl. Microwave uncovered for 3 minutes.

2   Add macaroni. Mix. Microwave uncovered for 5 minutes. Let it stand in hot water for 4-5 minutes. Drain and wash well with cold water.

3   In another microproof flat dish, microwave butter for 30 seconds.

4   Add oregano, spring onions, mushrooms and baby corns. Microwave uncovered for 5 minutes.

5   Add flour. Mix well and microwave uncovered for 30 seconds.

6   Add milk, salt, pepper & chilli flakes Mix and microwave uncovered for 6 minutes, stirring once inbetween. Microwave for 1-2 minutes more if the sauce does not turn thick.

7   Add macaroni, cream and ½ of grated cheese. Mix well. Arrange tomato, coriander and the left over grated cheese.

8   At serving time microwave uncovered for 2 minutes. Serve.

Chicken Stroganoff

Chicken combined with mushrooms in a creamy tomato - yogurt sauce.

Serves 4

INGREDIENTS

400 gm chicken - cut into ½" pieces

4 tbsp butter

1 small onion - chopped

150 gm mushrooms - cut into 2 halves

1½ tbsp maida (plain flour)

1 tbsp tomato puree

½ tbsp ketchup

½ tsp Worcestershire sauce

3-4 flakes garlic - crushed

½ tsp salt

¼ tsp pepper & chilli powder

¾ cup cream, 2 tbsp cheese spread

1 capsicum - cut into ½" cubes

METHOD

1   Sprinkle ½ tsp each of - salt, pepper and chilli powder over the chicken pieces. Mix well. Keep aside.

2   Put 2 tbsp butter in a microproof dish and microwave for 40 seconds.

3   Add onion & mushroom. Microwave for 3 minutes. Remove onion & mushroom from the dish.

4   In the same dish add 2 tbsp butter and chicken pieces and microwave covered for 4 minutes.

5   Add 1½ cups of water, 1 tbsp flour tomato puree, tomato ketchup, Worcestershire sauce, crushed garlic, salt, pepper and chilli powder. Microwave for 6 minutes or till slightly thick.

6   Whip cream and cheese spread well so that there are no lumps and it becomes smooth. Add cream-cheese mixture. Mix well. Add capsicum. Microwave for 2 minutes and serve hot with steamed rice sprinkled with chopped parsley.

Chicken & Sweet Corn

Chicken deliciously combined with sweet corn kernels and baked to perfection.

Serves 4

INGREDIENTS

300 gm boneless chicken- cut into slices

3 tbsp butter

1½ cups milk

½ cup sweet corn kernels (tinned)

2 spring onions - cut white part into rings and green into thin diagonal slices

1 potato - peeled & cut into ½" pieces

2 tbsp flour

½ cup grated cheese

1 tsp salt

½ tsp pepper

METHOD

1 Melt butter for 50 seconds in a microproof dish.

2 Add the chicken pieces and chopped potatoes. Microwave covered for 5 minutes or till cooked.

3 Add ¼ tsp salt and ¼ tsp pepper. Remove chicken and potatoes from the microproof dish and keep aside.

4 Melt butter for 50 seconds in the same dish.

5 Add white of spring onions and microwave for 2 minutes.

6 Add the tinned corn, flour & green spring onions. Mix well. Microwave for 40 seconds.

7 Add milk, salt and pepper. Microwave for 6 minutes or till slightly thickened. Stir once in between.

8 Mix chicken and potatoes. Sprinkle grated cheese.

9 Set your microwave oven at 180°C using the oven (convection) mode and press start to preheat oven.

10 Put the dish in the hot oven. Set the preheated oven for 15 minutes. Bake till golden brown. Serve hot.

Bean Casserole

Red kidney beans and cauliflower baked in a creamy cheese sauce.

Serves 6

INGREDIENTS

1¼ cups boiled rajmah (red kidney beans)

1 onion - chopped

4 cups finely chopped cauliflower

3 tomatoes

2½ tbsp tomato ketchup

1 tsp Worcestershire sauce

1½ cups (150 gm) grated cheese

½ cup cream

2 tbsp oil

salt and pepper to taste

METHOD

1. Put the tomatoes on a microproof plate and microwave for 3 minutes. Remove peel after they cool. Chop finely.

2. Keep onions, cauliflower and 2 tbsp oil in a microproof dish. Mix well and microwave for 6 minutes.

3. Add 1 tsp salt and ½ tsp pepper. Add tomatoes, boiled rajmah, ketchup and worcestershire sauce. Mix well. Check salt and pepper.

4. Add half of the grated cheese.

5. Mix the other half of the cheese with cream. Add ¼ tsp salt and ¼ tsp pepper. Pour cream over the vegetables and spread gently.

6. Set microwave oven at 180°C using the oven (convection) mode and press start to preheat oven. Put the vegetables inside the hot oven and re-set the preheated oven again at 180°C for 25 minutes. Bake till golden brown. Serve hot.

Hungarian Paneer

Cottage cheese slices layerd with vegetables, topped with a creamy tomato sauce flavoured with oregano.

Serves 8

INGREDIENTS

700-800 gm paneer - cut into a long, thick slab (7" long and 2" thick, approx.)

FILLING (MIX TOGETHER)

¾ cup grated carrot, 1 tbsp chopped olives

50 gm pizza cheese + 50 gm cheddar cheese - grated (1 cup)

¼ tsp salt & ¼ tsp freshly ground pepper

½ tsp oregano, or to taste

HUNGARIAN SAUCE

5 tomatoes, 6 tbsp ready made tomato puree, 2 tbsp oil

1 tsp crushed garlic, 4 tbsp cream

1 tsp oregano

½ tsp salt and ¼ tsp pepper, or to taste

METHOD

1   For sauce, prick tomatoes with a fork. Put on a microproof plate and microwave for 3 minutes. Remove peel. Blend to a puree after they cool down.

2   Put oil, garlic, 6 tbsp readymade puree, prepared puree, oregano, salt and pepper in a microproof bowl. Mix & microwave for 7 minutes.

3   Mix cream. Keep the sauce aside.

4   Cut paneer into 3 pieces lengthwise, of equal thickness. Sprinkle salt and pepper on both sides of each slice of paneer.

5   In a shallow rectangular serving dish, put ¼ of the prepared sauce.

6   Place a paneer slab on the sauce.

7   Spread ½ of the filling on it.

8   Press another piece of paneer on it.

9   Again put the filling on it. Cover with the last piece of paneer. Press. Pour sauce all over to cover top and sides completely. Grate cheese on top. Sprinkle some oregano or pepper. To serve, microwave for 3 minutes.

DESSERTS & CAKES

Gajar ka Halwa

Carrot pudding made in very little fat and in a jiffy too.

Serves 5-6

INGREDIENTS

½ kg carrots - grated

1½ cups milk

½ - ¾ cup sugar - powdered

½ cup (100 gms) khoya - grated

2-3 tbsp desi ghee

some chopped nuts like almonds, raisins (kishmish) etc.

METHOD

1   Mix grated carrots and milk in a big deep bowl.

2   Microwave uncovered for 15 minutes. Mix once after 5 minutes.

3   Add sugar and khoya. Mix well.

4   Microwave uncovered for 10 minutes.

5   Add ghee. Mix well. Microwave for 7 minutes. Mix chopped nuts. Serve hot or cold decorated with nuts.

Phirni

Rice pudding flavoured with green cardamoms and topped with nuts.

Serves 4

INGREDIENTS

3½ cups milk

¼ cup rice - soaked for 2-3 hours & ground to a fine paste

¼ cup powdered sugar, or to taste

1 tsp kewra or rose water - (optional) or a drop of kewra essence

seeds of 2-3 chhoti illaichi (green cardamom) - powdered

varak (silver leaf)

5-6 green pistas - sliced thinly

2 almonds - sliced into thin long pieces

METHOD

1   Soak rice in a little water for 2-3 hours. Grind in the mixer with a little water to a very fine paste.

2   In a dish mix ground rice and milk.

3   Microwave uncovered 6 minutes. Stir with a wire whisk, after every minute to prevent lumps formation. Break lumps if any.

4   Add sugar. Mix well. Microwave uncovered for 3 minutes, stirring in-between.

5   Mix well. Cool. Add rose/kewra water and illaichi powder. Pour in individual bowls.

6   Decorate with varak, nuts and illaichi powder. Serve chilled after 2-3 hours.

Pina Orange Dome

No cream! Pineapple and orange flavoured cheese icing makes this dessert quite low in calories.

Serves 12

INGREDIENTS

1 VANILLA CAKE OF 2 EGGS, PAGE 106

1 cup orange juice - to soak cake

5 cups chopped fresh ripe pineapple

8 tbsp powdered sugar

1 cup finely grated paneer (100 gm)

3 cups curd - hang for 30 minutes

1 orange and 5-6 almonds - to decorate

METHOD

1   To prepare vanilla cake, follow the recipe given for vanilla cake on page 106. Put cake batter in a dome shaped glass bowl. Microwave for 4 minutes. Let it cool.

2   Cut cake into 2 halves. Pour orange juice on both pieces to moisten cake.

3   Microwave 5 cups pineapple pieces with powdered sugar for 8 minutes or till it boils. Stir after a boil. Microwave for another 4-5 minutes. Let it cool. Keep ½ cup pineapple aside and puree the remaining in a mixer.

4   Remove ½ of the puree in a bowl. Add hung curd to it and mix well.

5   To the left over puree in the mixer, add paneer, churn till very smooth. Remove from blender to the bowl. Mix well with the curd - pineapple mixture. Add more sugar as needed.

6   Spread 2 tbsp pineapple topping on one piece of cake placed on the serving platter. Spread ½ cup finely chopped pineapple. Spread some topping on the other cake piece and invert on the first piece. Press.

7   Cover cake with left over topping.

8   Cut orange segments into half lengthwise and arrange at the bottom. Decorate with almonds.

Coconut Pudding

Coconut cake batter spread over sweetened apple and baked.

Serves 8

INGREDIENTS

½ kg apples - peeled, cut into ½" pieces

¼ cup plus ½ cup powdered sugar

½ cup butter - softened

1 cup flour maida (plain flour)

1 tsp baking powder

½ cup desiccated coconut powder

2 tbsp raisins, 2 eggs

1 tsp vanilla essence

½ cup milk

TOPPING

1 tbsp melted butter

2 tbsp brown sugar

METHOD

1   Mix apples with ¼ cup sugar and 1 tbsp butter in a microproof dish. Microwave for 4 minutes. Check sugar and add more as per taste. Keep aside.

2   Sift flour & baking powder. Add coconut powder and raisins.

3   Separate egg whites in a dry bowl. Beat till stiff peaks form. Keep aside.

4   In a big mixing bowl, beat butter and ½ cup powdered sugar until light and fluffy.

5   Add egg yolks and essence. Mix well.

6   Add flour mix & milk into the butter mixture. Beat well to get a soft dropping consistency.

7   Gently fold the beaten egg whites with a spoon into the pudding mixture. Spread over the fruit. Sprinkle brown sugar and some melted butter.

8   Bake in a pre-heated oven on convec mode at 180°C for 30 minutes or until firm to touch. Remove from oven. Serve pudding with hot or cold custard or cream.

Lychee Pearls in Shahi Kheer

Lychees are covered with silver leaf to make them look like pearls.

Serves 4-5

INGREDIENTS

10 fresh or canned lychees

10 almonds - blanched

3-4 sheets of varak (silver sheets)

SHAHI KHEER

3 cups milk (½ kg), 1 cup boiled rice

¼ tin condensed milk

1 cup grated paneer

10 almonds - cut into thin long pieces

1 tbsp kishmish, 1-2 drops kewra essence

seeds of 2 chhoti illaichi (green cardamoms) - powdered

DECORATION

¼ tsp kesar (saffron) - soaked in 1 tsp warm water

a few rose petals

METHOD

1   Microwave 3 cups milk and boiled rice in a big deep bowl for 8 minutes or till it boils.

2   Microwave at 60% power for 20 minutes, stirring once in between. Remove from microwave. Mash rice well.

3   Add all the other ingredients of the shahi kheer. Transfer to a shallow serving dish. Keep to chill in the fridge.

4   Remove seeds of lychees carefully. Insert an almond in each.

5   Place 3-4 lychees on a varak at intervals. Pick up the varak along with the lychees carefully such as to coat 3-4 lychees with one sheet of varak. Keep in the fridge.

6   At serving time, arrange the pearl lychees on the kheer. Dot with some kesar and sprinkle 1-2 rose petals.

Creme Caramel

The addition of a little custard powder in the mixture makes a world of difference to the caramel custard.

Serves 6

INGREDIENTS

2½ cups milk

8 tsp sugar

3 tbsp milk powder

1 tsp vanilla custard powder

3 eggs

1 tsp vanilla essence

3 tbsp sugar - to caramelize

METHOD

1   Mix milk with sugar, milk powder and custard powder till smooth in a deep microproof bowl and microwave for 10 minutes, stirring once or twice inbetween after 5 minutes. Let it cool.

2   Beat eggs and essence well with an egg beater till light and fluffy and add to the cooled milk. Keep aside.

3   Melt 3 tbsp sugar in a kadhai on low heat till golden. Pour in 6 small individual heat proof glass or metal bowls. Let the sugar set for 5 minutes.

4   Pour the milk-egg mixture in the moulds. Cover with aluminium foil.

5   Preheat the oven at 200°C using the oven (convec) mode. Bake pudding in the pre-heated oven on convec mode at 200°C for 20-25 minutes until firm and golden. Keep in the fridge so that it gets cold and sets. Do not unmould till it turns cold.

6   To serve, run a knife all around the mould and invert it on a plate. Give a slight jerk to unmould the pudding.

Vanilla Cake

A quick microwaved vanilla cake which can be had plain, or used for preparing any cake dessert.

Serve 4-5

INGREDIENTS

2 large eggs

½ cup powdered sugar (sugar has to be powdered, otherwise it burns)

½ cup maida, 1 tsp baking powder

¼ cup milk

½ cup oil

1 tsp vanilla essence

METHOD

1   Sift flour with baking powder. Keep aside.

2   Beat eggs and sugar till the eggs turn fluffy and the mixture becomes more than double in volume. Add essence.

3   Add oil to beaten egg-sugar mixture in the bowl. Mix well.

4   Fold in flour gradually till all the flour is used. Add milk to get a slightly thinner than a soft dropping consistency.

5   Grease a deep bowl. Pour the batter in it. Microwave uncovered for 4 minutes. Do not microwave for a longer time even if the surface of the cake does not feel firm and it appears wet after 4 minutes. Let it stand for 4-5 minutes. Let it cool 5-10 minutes before removing from baking dish.

Chocolate Cake

To convert a vanilla cake into a chocolate cake, add 2 tbsp cocoa powder and 2 extra tbsp powdered sugar to the recipe of vanilla cake given above. After the cake is ready, pour some chocolate sauce on it and serve.

Eggless Cake with Mocha Icing

A quick microwaved eggless chocolate cake topped with chocolate icing flavoured with coffee.

Serves 6

INGREDIENTS

½ tin condensed milk (milk-maid)

½ cup milk, ½ cup (75 gm) butter

1½ tbsp powdered sugar

100 gms (1 cup) maida (plain flour)

¼ cup cocoa, ¾ tsp level soda-bicarb

¾ tsp level baking powder

1 tsp vanilla essence, ¼ cup aerated soda

MOCHA GLAZE ICING

4 tbsp cocoa powder, 2 tbsp butter - softened

1 tsp coffee, 1 cup icing sugar - sifted

2-3 tbsp chopped walnuts (akhrot)

TO SOAK - ¼ cup coke or any other cola

METHOD

1   Sift maida with cocoa, soda-bicarb and baking powder. Keep aside.

2   Mix sugar and butter. Beat till very fluffy. Add milk-maid. Beat well.

3   Add milk and essence. Add maida. Beat well for 3-4 minutes till the mixture is smooth and light. Add soda and mix quickly. Transfer to a big, greased deep dish of 9" diameter.

4   Microwave for 5 minutes. Let it cool.

5   Cut cake into 2 & soak with cola drink.

6   For the icing, microwave 4 tbsp water in a bowl for 1 minute. Add coffee and mix. Add cocoa and butter to it and mix well. Return to microwave and microwave at 70% power for 1 minute or till butter melts. Gradually add the sifted icing sugar. Mix well.

7   Glaze the cake with the icing, making peaks with the spoon. Decorate it with walnuts.

8   Refrigerate until glaze is set. Serve with ice cream.

HEALTHY OLIVE OIL RECIPES

Mini Corn Buns

*Mini buns for little hands to hold with confidence, and a delicious mix of cheese,
paneer and veggies to fill hungry stomachs!*

Makes 12

INGREDIENTS

12 mini buns

4 tbsp olive oil

1 onion - finely chopped

¾ cup chopped cabbage

½ red capsicum - cubed

½ cup frozen corn

1 cheese cube - cut into tiny pieces

½ cup tiny pieces of paneer

1 tbsp chopped coriander

salt, pepper, oregano, to taste

MIX TOGETHER

3 tbsp cheese spread

3 tbsp thick yogurt

2 tsp tomato ketchup

2 tsp chilli garlic spread

METHOD

1   Hollow buns. Mix 2 tbsp olive oil with ¼ tsp each of salt, pepper and oregano. Brush the outside and inside of each bun with it. Keep aside.

2   Microwave 2 tbsp olive oil and onion for 4 minutes. Add cabbage, red capsicum and corn. Mix well. Add ¾ tsp salt, ½ tsp pepper and ½ tsp oregano. Add coriander leaves, paneer and cheese. Mix well.

3   Mix cheese spread with thick yogurt, ketchup and chilli garlic spread in a separate bowl.

4   Add vegetables to yogurt mix and check salt. Stuff in the buns and grill in a oven on the rack for 5 minutes till edges start to turn golden. Serve hot.

Baby Corn Jalfrazie

A baked dish for the Indian taste.

Serves 4

INGREDIENTS

12 baby corns - cut into half lengthwise

1 cup paneer - cut into (1"long) strips

2 tbsp oilve oil

2 onions - chopped

½ tsp onion seeds (kalonji), ½ tsp cumin seeds (jeera)

1/8 tsp asafoetida

½ tsp coriander seeds (saboot dhania) - crushed

1 tsp ginger-green chilli paste

2 spring onions - sliced diagonally, keep greens separate

½ green capsicum - sliced, ½ red capsicum - sliced

½ tsp chilli powder, ½ tsp salt

½ tsp bhuna jeera powder

TOMATO MASALA

2 tbsp olive oil

2 tbsp tomato ketchup

½ cup ready-made tomato puree

2 tbsp chopped green coriander, salt, pepper to taste

METHOD

1   Microwave olive oil, cumin, onion seeds (kalonji), asafoetida (hing), chopped onions and crushed saboot dhania. Microwave for 7 minutes. Add ginger-green chilli paste. Mix. Add ¼ cup water and mix.

2   Add baby corns, spring onion, red and green capsicums. Mix well. Microwave for 5 minute.

3   Add paneer, red chilli powder, salt and bhuna jeera powder. Mix well. Keep aside.

4   For the tomato masala, microwave olive oil with ready-made tomato puree, ketchup, pepper and salt for 4 minutes. Add chopped coriander and the baby corns with paneer. Mix gently. To serve, microwave for 2 minutes.

Mushroom Olive Baskets

You can even add peppers, baby corn or any other vegetables you like along with the mushrooms.

Makes 9 baskets

INGREDIENTS

9 slices of bread, 2 tbsp olive oil

¼ tsp chilli flakes, ¼ tsp oregano

TOPPING

2 cups chopped mushrooms (use stems also)

2 tbsp olive oil, ½ onion - finely chopped

½ green chilli - finely chopped

2 tsp plain flour (maida)

½ cup milk, 1 cheese cube - grated

¼ tsp mustard sauce

4-6 black olives- deseeded and chopped

2 tbsp chopped parsley/coriander

½ tsp salt and ¼ tsp pepper to taste

METHOD

1   Keep the bread on a flat rolling board. With the help of a rolling pin (belan), press applying pressure and roll out the bread to make it thin. Take a big cookie cutter or a big steel katori. Cut out a round bigger than the muffin cup so that the bread basket can get folds. Repeat with all slices.

2   Mix olive oil with chilli flakes and oregano and brush this oil on all round pieces of bread. Pick up a round piece of bread from the sides and place in the greased muffin tray in each cup. Grill the bread basket in the preheated oven for 6-7 minutes or till evenly browned on the edges.

3   For the filling, microwave olive oil, onion, green chilli and mushrooms for 5 minutes. Add flour. Mix well and microwave uncovered for 30 seconds. Add milk, mix and microwave for 3 minutes, stirring once in between.

4   Add the parsley or coriander, cheese, mustard, black olives, salt and pepper and mix well. Keep aside.

5   At the time of serving, fill the baskets with the filling. Grill for 3-4 minutes.

Herb Bread Loaf

Learn how to make fresh-baked bread at home – this loaf is filled with herbs and topped with tomatoes and olives.

Serves 6

INGREDIENTS

1 cup whole wheat flour (atta), 1 cup plain flour (maida)

½ tsp each of dried herbs - oregano, parsley, red chilli flakes

3 tsp dry yeast or 6 tsp fresh yeast

1 tsp salt

1 tsp sugar

2 tbsp olive oil

¼ cup milk

TOPPING

1 tomato - cut into slices, a few black olives - sliced

2 tbsp chopped fresh parsley

1 tsp poppy seeds (khus khus) to sprinkle

1 tbsp olive oil mixed with 2 tbsp warm milk

METHOD

1. Put warm water in a bowl. Add sugar and yeast. Cover and keep aside for 15 minutes till frothy and it rises.

2. Sift flour in a big mixing bowl. Add all herbs. Add frothy yeast, salt and olive oil to flour. Mix it nicely. Add about ½ cup warm water gradually and knead with your palms till smooth and no longer sticky. Keep kneading with wet hands to get a soft and smooth dough.

3. To make it elastic put the dough on a lightly floured platform. Push the dough forward with your palms, fold over towards you with the fingers and push again with the palm. Give the dough a turn and knead again. Knead till very smooth for about 10 minutes. You can knead the dough in the food processor. Put dough in a bowl. Cover with a cling film. Keep aside to prove for about 1½ hours till double in size.

4. Punch dough lightly. Put it in a big, well greased loaf tin. Level it. Top with tomatoes, olives. Keep for final proofing for 20 minutes.

5. Brush with milk and olive oil. Sprinkle parsley and poppy seeds. Bake in a preheated oven at 210°C for about 20 minutes, until light golden from the top.

Cottage Cheese Steaks

The vegetarians going to love this simple continental dish of paneer.

Serves 4

INGREDIENTS

200 gms paneer - cut into 2" squares or rectangles of ½" thickness

4 tbsp olive oil

4 tbsp finely grated parmesan cheese or cheddar cheese

½ tsp salt

¼ tsp pepper

4 tbsp chopped fresh basil leaves or fresh coriander

500 gm (6) tomatoes

1 tsp chopped garlic

1 small onion - chopped finely

1 tsp sugar

½ tsp chilli flakes

1 tsp salt

METHOD

1   Mix salt, pepper, 2 tbsp olive oil and basil or coriander. Add cheese. Keep aside.

2   Wash & microwave covered whole tomatoes for 7 minutes. Cool and blend to a puree.

3   Microwave 2 tbsp olive with garlic and onion for 4 minutes. Add fresh tomato puree, salt, sugar and chilli flakes. Microwave covered for 10 minutes till a slightly thick sauce is ready. Stir once in between.

4   Brush the paneer slices on both sides with the cheese -olive oil mixture and put under a preheated grill for 5 minutes. Turn and grill for 2 minutes. Do not over cook and harden the paneer.

5   To serve, place most of the tomato sauce in flat dish or platter. Arrange steaks. Sprinkle the remaining sauce on the steaks. Microwave for 1 minute.

Quick Tandoori Platter

The pineapple adds a twist to this platter.

Serves 6

INGREDIENTS

200 gm paneer - cut into ¾"-1" cubes (14-16 pieces)

1 green capsicum - cut into 1" pieces

1 red capsicum or tomato - cut into 1" cubes (deseed tomatoes)

1 large onion - cut into 8 pieces

6 baby potatoes - boiled and peeled, optional

2 fresh pineapple slices - each cut into 4-6 pieces

MARINADE

1 tbsp gram flour (besan)

2 tbsp lemon juice

3 tbsp olive oil

1 tbsp tandoori masala

1 tsp chaat masala

1 tsp salt

½ tsp garam masala

½ tsp degi mirch

2 tsp ginger-green chilli paste

METHOD

1   Mix besan with oil & lemon juice to a smooth paste in a bowl. Add all the other ingredients of the marinade. Add veggies, pineapple & paneer & mix gently to coat.

2   To serve, cover a grill rack with foil & grease it. Place all vegetables, pineapple & paneer on it. Grill for 10-12 minutes in a preheated grill.

Spinach Paneer Casserole

Paneer topped with roasted tomatoes on a bed of spinach.

Serves 4-5

INGREDIENTS

200 gm paneer - cut into ¼" cubes

1 tsp oregano

2 tbsp olive oil

1 onion - chopped finely

3 tsp chopped garlic

½ kg spinach - shred leaves finely

1-2 green chillies - chopped finely

2 cups milk

3 tsp cornflour

½ tsp cinnamon (dalchini) powder

½ tsp black pepper

1 tsp salt

TOMATO TOPPING

2 tbsp olive oil, 1 tomato - chopped

1 onion - finely chopped, ½ cup tomato puree

½ tsp salt

1 tbsp chopped fresh coriander, a pinch sugar

METHOD

1   Microwave 2 tbsp olive oil, onions and garlic for 3 minutes. Wash and add spinach and green chillies and microwave for 6 minutes.

2   Dissolve cornflour, cinnamon, black pepper and salt in milk and add to the cooked spinach. Microwave for about 6 minutes till slightly thick.

3   In a greased baking dish pour the spinach mixture. Spread the paneer pieces over it. Sprinkle oregano.   Keep aside.

4   To prepare the tomato topping, microwave olive oil and onion for 4 minutes. Add other ingredients and microwave for 4 minutes.

5   Spread the tomato topping on the paneer in the dish. Bake covered with foil at 180°C for 10-12 minutes. Serve hot with a bread.

Baked Yogurt Wheels

These pinwheel style pieces are fun to eat.

Serves 4

INGREDIENTS

4 slices of soft fresh bread

1-2 tsp mustard sauce - to spread, optional

2-3 tbsp milk

½ tsp carom seeds (ajwain)

FILLING

½ cup curd - hang for 1 hour in a muslin cloth and squeeze

2 tbsp finely chopped red capsicum or deseeded tomato

1 cup finely chopped broccoli

2 tbsp peas

1 green chilli - deseeded & finely chopped

½ tsp salt

½ tsp pepper

¼ tsp red chilli flakes

METHOD

1 Wash and microwave broccoli & peas for 2 minutes. Mash peas with the hands. Strain.

2 Put the hung curd in a bowl. Add all other ingredients of the filling to the curd and mix. Keep aside.

3 Cut the sides of a slice, keep it flat on a rolling board. Press, applying pressure with a belan so that holes of the bread close. (You can microwave the bread slice for a few seconds before rolling.) Spread ½ tsp mustard on it.

4 Spread a layer of filling. Roll carefully. Seal end by applying some curd. Press well.

5 Brush milk on roll. Spread some carom seeds on a plate and roll the bread roll over it. Gently cut each roll into 2 pieces.

6 At serving time, cover a grill rack of oven with foil. Grease foil lightly. Place wheels. Grill for about 6 minutes till edges turn golden. Serve immediately.

Rice & Corn Salad

A great combination of vegetables and rice.

Serves 4

INGREDIENTS

¾ cup boiled rice - refrigerate for 2 hours

1 tbsp olive oil

1 small cucumber - washed and chopped with the peel (1 cup)

1 cup corn

6-8 medium florets of broccoli

4-5 black olives, 4-5 slices of pickled jalapenos

½ tsp salt, ½ tsp pepper, ½ tsp oregano, 2 tbsp lemon juice

TEMPERING

1 tbsp olive oil

1 onion - sliced

2-3 tbsp finely chopped parsley, ¼ tsp salt

1 tbsp chopped walnuts

2 tbsp thickly grated fresh coconut

METHOD

1   Drizzle 1 tbsp olive oil on cooked rice and separate rice grains with a fork. Wash broccoli florets and microwave for 2 minutes. Pat dry and keep aside to cool.

2   To the rice, add cucumber, corn, broccoli, olives and jalapenos. Sprinkle salt, pepper and lemon juice. Mix gently.

3   For tempering, microwave olive oil and onion for 5 minutes till golden brown. Add all the remaining ingredients and mix well. Microwave for 1 minute.

4   Pour tempering over the rice mixture. Mix lightly. Serve at room temperature.

Grilled Cheesy Bites

*A child-friendly, small-sized bread base has a rich cheesy topping,
scattered with multicoloured gems – tiny cubes of veggies.*

Serves 6-8

INGREDIENTS

1 small french loaf or bread

2 tbsp olive oil, chilli flakes and oregano to sprinkle

TOPPING

½ cup grated cheddar cheese, ½ cup grated paneer

4 tbsp mayonnaise

2 tsp mustard sauce

2 tsp tomato ketchup

½ tsp chilli flakes, ½ tsp oregano

¼ tsp pepper, 2 pinches of salt

1 onion - chopped finely

½ green capsicum - chopped finely

1 small tomato - deseeded & finely chopped (cut a tomato into 4 pieces & remove pulp)

¼ cup chopped cabbage

2 tbsp corn kernels, optional

2 tbsp chopped coriander leaves

METHOD

1   Cut the french bread into ½" thick slices. Brush with olive oil. Sprinkle red chili flakes and oregano. Grill with the oil side up for about 4 minutes till golden brown.

2   Mix together cheese, paneer, mayonnaise, mustard, ketchup, salt, pepper, chilli flakes and oregano.

3   Add all the other ingredients of the topping and mix lightly.

4   Pile the topping on the untoasted side of the bread.

5   Place bread under a grill for 3-4 minutes and grill till light golden. Serve immediately.

Veggie Pepper Rice

Healthy pepper flavoured rice with vegetables.

Serves 2

INGREDIENTS

1 cup rice - soaked for 15-20 minutes

3 tbsp olive oil

8-10 pepper corns

1 onion - sliced

1 capsicum

4-5 beans and 1 carrot - chopped

1 tsp salt

½ tsp freshly crushed pepper

½-1 tsp soya sauce

METHOD

1   Mix olive oil, pepper corns, onion, capsicum, beans, carrot in a big flat microproof dish and microwave for 4 minutes.

2   Drain rice. Add rice, 2 cups water, salt, pepper & soya sauce. Mix well. Microwave covered for 13 minutes. Stir once in between.

3   Sprinkle crushed pepper. Serve after 5 minutes.

Creamed Corn Chillies

An unusual recipe. Hot yet delicious!

Makes 10

10 big, thick dark green chillies with stem (250 gm)

1 tbsp olive oil

MARINADE

3 tbsp lemon juice, 3 tbsp white vinegar, ½ tsp garlic paste, ½ tsp salt, 1 tsp sugar

STUFFING

½ tin cream style sweet corn (1 cup)

2 tbsp olive oil

1 onion - chopped finely

½ tsp crushed garlic

1 tsp tomato ketchup

½ tsp salt, ¼ tsp pepper

1 tsp white vinegar¼ tsp white pepper

1 cheese cube - diced into tiny pieces

METHOD

1   Cut a slit lengthwise in each chilli, leaving the edges intact to hold the filling well. Scoop out the seeds completely with the help of a knife.

2   Mix all the ingredients of the marinade in a bowl. Put 1 tbsp of marinade in each chilli, shake it well and remove the marinade to the bowl to reuse it. Similarly do with all chillies. Place chillies in a single layer in a plate. Microwave for 4 minutes.

3   For the stuffing, mix olive oil, garlic and onion in flate dish. Microwave for 3 minutes.

4   Add cream style corn, ketchup, salt, pepper and vinegar. Microwave for 3 minutes or till dry.

5   Remove from oven and add cheese cubes.

6   Stuff the chillies with this filling. They should be stuffed well but not to bursting point. Rub olive oil on the stuffed chillies.

7   To serve, place the chillies on a greased wire rack or on a non-stick tawa available with the microwave. If using the non stick tawa, place it on the grill rack in the oven. Grill the chillies for 6-8 minutes in a preheated grill, turning once in between if needed.

NITA MEHTA COOK BOOKS

101 Recipes for
CHILDREN

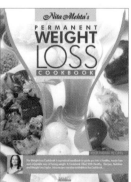

Permanent
WEIGHT LOSS Cookbook

101 INTERNATIONAL
Recipes

101 NON-VEGETARIAN
Recipes

101 VEGETARIAN
Recipes

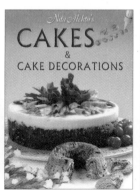

CAKES
& Cake Decorations

ZERO OIL
Cooking

Cooking for
GROWING CHILDREN

AMRITSARI
Khaana

SIZZLERS
Cookbook

Best of
INDIAN COOKING

INDIAN FAVOURITES
(Veg. & Non-Veg.)